MARGARET MEA.

Anthropology's Ancestors

Edited by Aleksandar Bošković, University of Belgrade; Institute of Archaeology, Belgrade; Max Planck Institute for Social Anthropology, Halle/Saale

As anthropology developed across geographical, historical, and social boundaries, it was always influenced by works of exceptional scholars who pushed research topics in new and original directions and who can be regarded as important ancestors of the discipline. The aim of this series is to offer introductions to these major figures, whose works constitute landmarks and are essential reading for students of anthropology, but who are also of interest for scholars in the humanities and social sciences more generally. In doing so, it offers important insights into some of the basic questions facing humanity.

Volume 1
Margaret Mead
Paul Shankman

Volume 2
William Robertson Smith
Aleksandar Bošković

MARGARET
MEAD

• • •

Paul Shankman

berghahn
NEW YORK • OXFORD
www.berghahnbooks.com

First published in 2021 by
Berghahn Books
www.berghahnbooks.com

Library of Congress Cataloging-in-Publication Data

Names: Shankman, Paul, author.
Title: Margaret Mead / Paul Shankman.
Description: New York: Berghahn Books, 2021. | Series:
  Anthropology's Ancestors; volume 1 | Includes bibliographical
  references and index.
Identifiers: LCCN 2021020961 (print) | LCCN 2021020962 (ebook) |
  ISBN 9781800731417 (hardback) | ISBN 9781800731424 (ebook)
Subjects: LCSH: Mead, Margaret, 1901–1978. | Women
  anthropologists—United States—Biography.
Classification: LCC GN21.M36 S53 2021 (print) | LCC GN21.M36
  (ebook) | DDC 301.092 [B]—dc23
LC record available at https://lccn.loc.gov/2021020961
LC ebook record available at https://lccn.loc.gov/2021020962

British Library Cataloguing in Publication Data

A catalogue record for this book is available from the British Library

ISBN 978-1-80073-141-7 hardback
ISBN 978-1-80073-143-1 paperback
ISBN 978-1-80073-142-4 ebook

To Nash, Noa, and Elijah

CONTENTS

•   •   •

FIGURES

* * *

ACKNOWLEDGMENTS

* * *

Biographies such as this rely on earlier work, and there is much fine work about Margaret Mead on which to draw. Books by Jane Howard (1984), Mary Catherine Bateson (1984), Hilary Lapsley (1999), Lois Banner (2003), Nancy Lutkehaus (2009), and Peter Mandler (2013) provide much of the background for this biography. In addition, Mead's autobiography (1972), her extensive publications, her letters, and the many commentaries on her life and work by anthropologists and others have been very helpful. Readers may consult the notes at the end of each chapter and bibliography to get a sense of how much good scholarship is available.

Tracy Ehlers, Judith Schachter, Herbert Lewis, and Sally Shankman read earlier versions of the book manuscript and provided valuable comments. They are in no way responsible for the content or views shared within. My colleagues in the Association for Social Anthropology in Oceania and the many Samoans who have assisted in my understanding of their culture deserve recognition too.

I would also like to thank Tom Bonnington and Aleksandar Bošković, who encouraged me to author this biography for the Berghahn Books series on anthropology's ancestors. Initially, I thought that capturing Mead's life and work in a short biography would be impossible. After all, Jane Howard's biography of Mead is over 500 pages in length. Although not impossible, synthesizing and condensing Mead's life and work into a short biography has been a challenge, quite simply because Margaret Mead was such a remarkable person and scholar.

Portions of chapters 1, 2, and 3 draw heavily on my book, *The Trashing of Margaret Mead: Anatomy of an Anthropological Con-*

troversy, and are reprinted by permission of the University of Wisconsin Press (copyright 2009) by the Board of Regents of the University of Wisconsin System. All rights reserved.

Chapter 10 draws heavily on my article, "The Public Anthropology of Margaret Mead: *Redbook*, Women's Issues, and the 1960s." *Current Anthropology* 59(1): 55–73, and substantial portions are reprinted by permission of the Wenner-Gren Foundation for Anthropological Research (copyright 2018). All rights reserved.

Chapter 11, note 1 draws on my article, "The 'Fateful Hoaxing' of Margaret Mead: A Cautionary Tale." *Current Anthropology* 54(1): 51–69, and portions are reprinted by permission of the Wenner-Gren Foundation for Anthropological Research (copyright 2013). All rights reserved.

INTRODUCTION

• • •

At the time of her death in 1978, Margaret Mead was one of the three best-known women in the United States and America's first woman of science. A prolific author, sought-after public speaker, icon, and oracle, Mead was the public face of anthropology and its ambassador to the world for much of the twentieth century. She spoke to the great issues of her time and was widely recognized for her many contributions. After her death, she was awarded the Presidential Medal of Freedom by President Jimmy Carter. The award noted that

> Margaret Mead was both a student of civilization and an exemplar of it. To a public of millions, she brought the central insight of cultural anthropology: that varying cultural patterns express an underlying human unity. She mastered her discipline, but she also transcended it. Intrepid, independent, plain spoken, fearless, she remains a model for the young and a teacher from whom all may learn.

On the other side of the world, Mead's passing was remembered in a very different context. On the island of Manus off the coast of New Guinea, the people of Pere village also mourned her death. Mead first studied the people of Pere in the late 1920s, returning in the 1950s with further visits thereafter. Over a span of five decades, she touched their lives, and they touched hers. Such was Mead's stature that they commemorated her death with a ceremony befitting a great leader.

* * *

Who was Margaret Mead? And how did she become such an exceptional anthropologist and public figure? Mead began her career in anthropology with graduate work at Columbia University and fieldwork in Samoa in the 1920s. Public recognition came with her very first book, *Coming of Age in Samoa* (1928b). But Samoa was just the beginning of a long and very productive career. On her return from the islands, Mead became an assistant curator at the American Museum of Natural History in New York City, home for her entire professional life. She spent much of the next decade doing more fieldwork in the South Pacific as a committed and indefatigable ethnographer. Between 1928 and 1939, Mead conducted fieldwork in five different New Guinea cultures, including Manus, Arapesh, Tchambuli, Mundugumor, and Iatmul, as well as additional fieldwork in Bali and on the Omaha reservation. No anthropologist has conducted as much fieldwork in as many different cultures in such a brief period of time and published as much professional and popular work on them as Mead did. She was a whirlwind of energy and professional activity.

Mead pioneered work on topics such as childhood, adolescence, gender, and national character, and was a founding figure in culture-and-personality studies. She advanced fieldwork methods through the use of photography, film, and psychological testing, as well as the use of teams of researchers—women and men. Her popular books from this period include the bestsellers *Growing Up in New Guinea* (1930b) and *Sex and Temperament in Three Primitive Societies* (1935). She also authored professional monographs and articles on most of the cultures that she studied.

Mead was one of the three great popularizers of the concept of culture in the early decades of the twentieth century. Along with her mentors, Franz Boas and Ruth Benedict, she led a revolution in how people thought about differences between groups of people. This tiny band of anthropologists from a virtually unknown discipline had a major impact on academic and public thinking about "race." At the turn of the twentieth century, "race" and inborn biological traits were thought to explain differences between groups, and ideas about racial superiority and inferiority were part of this world view. The replacement of racial thinking with a cultural perspective on group differences was anthropology's most significant contribution in the first half of the twentieth century, and Mead was one of its foremost proponents.

Using Samoa as a case study, Mead found that culture, rather than biology, was responsible for differences between American and Samoan adolescents. According to Mead, Samoan adolescence was less stressful than American adolescence, and this was the result of socialization within a specific cultural context. American and Samoan adolescents shared a common biology, but biology was not destiny. So the same biological process—puberty—did not lead to similar behavioral outcomes. Moreover, these differences did not indicate the superiority of one group's socialization practices over another's.

Like other cultural anthropologists, Mead advocated temporarily suspending Western values and judgments in order to understand other cultures on their own terms. So, in the study of cultures, ethnocentrism gave way to cultural relativism. Today this perspective is taken for granted, but in the early twentieth century cultural relativism was an important step forward for ethnographers of that era and for the public. In addition, Mead used her own values and judgments in comparing cultures and in drawing lessons for American society from her study of other cultures; thus, the subtitle of *Coming of Age in Samoa* was *A Psychological Study of Primitive Youth for Western Civilisation*.

Following her ethnographic work in the 1920s and 1930s, Mead's career took a different direction with the onset of World War II. During the war, she worked for the U.S. government. Unlike her earlier, village-based fieldwork in non-Western cultures, Mead was now studying the national character of highly stratified, mostly Western nations. Since fieldwork was not possible during the war, interdisciplinary teams of researchers studied these cultures "at a distance." Mead was also involved in applied projects during the war and would become a founding member of the Society for Applied Anthropology. In the postwar era, Mead continued to network broadly across disciplinary boundaries, leading organizations, arranging conferences on pressing issues, and making anthropology relevant to audiences beyond her own field.

In 1960, Mead was elected president of the American Anthropological Association, and in 1975 she became president of the American Association for the Advancement of Science. As a public figure and influential thinker, she wrote for popular magazines, such as *Redbook*, and appeared on radio and television programs, as well as authored more bestselling books such as *Male and Female* (1949), *Culture and Commitment* (1971), and her autobiography *Blackberry Winter* (1972). People wanted to know what Margaret Mead would say, and she was quite willing to share her opinions. As a result, her colleagues in anthropology had mixed views about Mead. On the one hand, they appreciated her work in the public sphere, putting anthropology on the map. Yet that same work also led anthropologists to label her a "popularizer" and to pay less attention to the professional side of her work.

In the public eye, Mead was a complex figure. Her accomplishments led many Americans to admire her. *Time* magazine called her "Mother to the World" (21 March 1969). A number of young women saw Mead as a role model and early feminist. However, in the 1960s Mead did not consider herself a feminist and had harsh words for "radical" feminists. On the other hand, conservative critics sometimes viewed Mead as a dangerous liberal responsible for the sexual revolution and the subsequent "moral decay" of American youth. Yet a review of Mead's writing during the 1960s demonstrates that she was not in the forefront of either the sexual revolution or the women's movement.

Mead's life and work embodied many apparent contradictions, making her almost impossible to characterize or categorize. As Nancy Lutkehaus has written, Mead was *both*:

American intellectual and best-selling author/media celebrity, innovative ethnographer and popularizer of anthropology, dedicated social scientist and outspoken social critic, bourgeois liberal and staunch Episcopalian ... professional career woman and champion of motherhood, a successful

woman in a man's world, feminine and masculine, hetero-
sexual and homosexual. (Lutkehaus 2008: 8)

Similarly, there is no easy way to summarize Mead's contributions. A listing of her publications alone is the subject of a small
book (Gordan 1976). Indeed, Mead authored, coauthored, and
edited over three dozen books. Although not the most important theorist of her era, her pioneering research and writing laid
a foundation for work by future anthropologists and others; her
tireless efforts on anthropology's behalf helped Americans understand what anthropology was, and her ability to connect with
the public remains unparalleled.

This book traces Mead's career as an ethnographer, as an early
voice of anthropology, and as a public figure, linking the professional and personal sides of her career. Her personal network of
mentors, friends, partners, and spouses played a major role in
her career opportunities, field site choices, and theoretical perspectives. This network provides an important context for understanding Mead's career through the end of World War II, a
period that comprises much of this book. Samoa receives special
emphasis because it provided a template for her future fieldwork.
Mead's personal opinions about her ethnographic work during
the 1920s and 1930s have been included because she was unusually candid in providing a "behind-the-scenes" view of her life as
a fieldworker.

The latter part of the book focuses on Mead's work on national
character studies during and immediately after World War II, her
interdisciplinary work outside of anthropology, and her role as a
public figure up to her death. These areas of Mead's life are less
well known but were significant nonetheless. In these latter sections of the book, criticism of Mead's professional and popular
work will be discussed, including the controversy over *Coming of
Age in Samoa*. The final part of the book examines Mead's multiple legacies.

Readers may already be familiar with Mead and wish to learn
more. There is a great deal to learn. In doing research for this
book, I read or reread most of Mead's major works, a number

of her letters, as well as biographical works about her life. And I am still learning. Mead was unique as a scholar, activist, and person, accomplishing so much and doing so as a woman in a man's world. Her success in this predominantly male context, both within anthropology and beyond, cannot be overstated. Yet some of her work was ultimately unsuccessful, including the national character studies to which she devoted over a decade of her life. And there were personal relationships that did not turn out well. Addressing all of the dimensions of Mead's life and work is beyond the scope of this book. Nevertheless, I shall try to cover a number of them in this introduction to one of anthropology's most important ancestors.

CHAPTER 1

BEGINNINGS

●　●　●

At the turn of the twentieth century, the discipline of anthro-pology in the United States was in its infancy. Although there had been earlier associations of anthropologists, the American Anthropological Association was not founded until 1902 with an initial 175 members, most of whom were nonprofessionals. Early amateur anthropologists, such as Lewis Henry Morgan working among the Iroquois and Frank Cushing working among the Zuni, produced excellent studies. But in the early twentieth century, there were few university-based departments of anthropology, less than a handful of graduate programs in anthropology, and fewer than a dozen people with PhDs in anthropology. Most of the anthropology during this period was centered in museums, like the Smithsonian and the American Museum of Natural History, and in the Bureau of American Ethnology, a government-funded organization charged with research on the indigenous people of North America. Anthropology at this time was in the process of becoming a profession rather than being a discipline with a set of already-established norms.

In 1889, Franz Boas became an assistant professor at Clark University in Massachusetts; this was the first university-based appointment in anthropology in the United States. Boas was not trained in anthropology; he received a PhD in physics in Ger-many for his study of the optical properties of water. However, Boas had done ethnographic fieldwork among the Inuit of Baffin Island and on the Northwest Coast, and he would quite literally establish the new discipline of anthropology in the United States.

Boas would build the Department of Anthropology at Columbia University that, along with the Department of Anthropology at Harvard, would become one of the two major graduate programs in the early twentieth century. These and other programs were small, yielding a total of only fifty or so PhDs by the mid-1920s, but they were the training ground for a generation of young scholars like Margaret Mead.

Mead was born into a family of academics in 1901, the eldest of four surviving children. Her mother was a sociologist, a feminist, and author of two books. Her father taught business in the Wharton School at the University of Pennsylvania. Mead's family was unusual in its commitment to education, especially for women. Both Mead's mother and one of her grandmothers were professionals. And because they were professionals, it never occurred to Mead that she should confine herself to the roles of mother and homemaker as most women of her generation would.

Young Margaret loved the world of books, poetry, and ideas. Her family praised her intelligence. And she had a mind of her own. Although her parents were agnostics, at age eleven Margaret chose to become an Episcopalian, a religious faith that she maintained for her entire life. While in high school, Margaret met Luther Cressman, a college student four years her senior who planned to become a Lutheran minister. They fell in love and became engaged when she was sixteen. Margaret did not tell her parents about the engagement until sometime later. She also encouraged Cressman to leave the Lutheran faith and become an Episcopalian like herself. At this moment, Margaret thought she might live happily as a minister's wife and the mother of several children. However, their engagement would last five years, and during this period both Mead and Cressman would undergo major changes in their life goals.

Mead spent her first year of college at DePauw University in Indiana, the school that her father had attended. DePauw was a small liberal arts school, and Mead's experience there was difficult. She did not fit into the sorority system that dominated the lives of most young women. Although she attended sorority rush parties, she did not receive a bid to pledge. Her engagement to Cressman may have lessened the sting, but she nonetheless felt like an outsider, an outcast. Her clothes were not stylish enough for most of the other young women that she knew. Her intelligence, so highly valued by her family, was now a liability; the young men in her classes resented her for it. After class, Mead would read avidly about the literary and artistic scene in New York City, where Cressman was now living and studying. She became acutely aware of the constraints of DePauw, where she felt like "an exile" (Mead 1972: 107).

NEW YORK

In 1919, Mead transferred to Barnard, the women's college in New York City affiliated with Columbia University. Here her personal odyssey took a turn for the better. At Barnard, sororities had been abolished in 1913. In this new setting, Mead flourished, becoming involved with a progressive circle of friends and an exciting set of experiences. World War I was over, and the great flu pandemic of 1918–1919 had passed. In 1920, women earned the right to vote. This was the beginning of the Roaring Twenties, and if America had one city that exemplified this period, it was New York. There was art, poetry, literature, music, and alcohol (even though it was during Prohibition). There was great interest in politics and psychoanalysis. Bohemian, avant-garde, and the cultural epicenter of cosmopolitan America, New York seemed made for Mead. There was a world of ideas to be encountered, exchanged, and debated.

For Mead, Barnard was a liberating experience, intellectually and personally. Her close-knit group of friends, known to each other as the "Ash Can Cats," thought of themselves as "radicals," mostly in the cultural rather than the political sense. They engaged in lengthy discussions about sex, repression, pregnancy, marriage, and homosexuality. For Mead and her cohort, sexual politics were a matter of serious ethical concern. They read the new literature on the philosophy of free love and learned about sexual technique in manuals by influential authors such as Have-lock Ellis.

As a modern young woman, Mead embraced the idea of free love and promoted it in conversations with her fiancé and friends. On a philosophical level, Mead believed that free love meant following one's heart rather than conventional norms about commitment to one partner, marriage, and heterosexuality. If marriage and passion coincided, so much the better, but love itself was paramount. Free love also meant that multiple relationships were possible as well as homosexual relationships. Jealousy was considered a negative emotion because jealousy implied possessiveness and prevented free love. As an idea, free love appealed to Mead. It also became a matter of practical concern.

At Barnard, Mead was now intellectually exciting and attractive, especially among her female peers. She was also daring. While chaste in her ongoing engagement with Cressman, Mead explored lesbian relationships inside and outside her social circle. She enjoyed these relationships while keeping them secret. They were passionate, complicated, and left Mead feeling torn as she tried to manage them. Mead was initially uncertain about her own sexual orientation and troubled by it. Homosexuality was generally taboo, and bisexuality was even less well understood, although in the 1920s both were considered acceptable and even fashionable in some New York social circles.

ANTHROPOLOGY BECKONS

Apart from the personal issues that were so important in her development, Mead's academic abilities were now recognized, although her academic direction was shifting. She had wanted to be a writer, journalist, or poet, among other possibilities, but she switched her academic major from English at DePauw to psychology at Barnard, while contemplating philosophy in between. Mead was a quick study and an excellent student whose ability to process information was impressive. Yet at this time a very painful bout of neuritis in her right arm rendered her unable to write with that hand. Mead learned to write with her left hand and, when the neuritis subsided, she was able to write with both hands simultaneously. She could now take class notes with one hand and, if bored, write letters with the other (Francis 2001: 5).

Mead's interest in anthropology came late in her undergraduate career. In her senior year at Barnard, after committing to psychology, she took a course from Franz Boas. As a result of her upbringing, Mead already believed in the equality of "races" and that cultures were neither inherently superior nor inferior to each other. These ideas—a minority view at the time—were familiar to her. Boas also introduced Mead to the idea of human evolution, which strongly influenced her. In addition, she met Boas's teaching assistant, Ruth Benedict, who would become her close personal friend, colleague, and intellectual partner. Benedict was working on her own PhD dissertation, specializing in Native American cultures.

After taking one course from Boas, Mead attended all the others that he taught, and got to know Benedict better. Nevertheless, rather than applying for graduate work in anthropology, she entered the graduate program in psychology at Columbia, earning an MA in that field. At that time, psychology was the most important and most developed of the social sciences. Mead took a total of fifteen courses in psychology and educational psychology, as well as two sociology classes dealing with psychological aspects of culture, at Barnard, Columbia, and Teacher's College. These courses gave her a firm academic background in that discipline and practical experience administering psychological tests (Francis 2005).

Mead's master's thesis, "Intelligence Tests of Italian and American Children" (1924), was based on research in New Jersey among Italian immigrant children and demonstrated that cultural background, including language proficiency in English, influenced intelligence test scores. The tests were therefore not a measure of innate biological ability as many experts thought. Mead's interest in culture, her mentors and classes in psychology, and her ability to use psychological testing would assist her future work in Samoa and beyond, although she did not know it at the time.

At one of their lunches, Benedict, who was fifteen years older than Mead, told her that she and Boas hoped that Mead would pursue anthropology, but they had nothing to offer her except "the work itself," which could not wait because cultures around the world were rapidly disappearing. Mead had already made up her mind. Anthropology would become her career. Boas became her mentor and advisor; Benedict was also a mentor.

Mead's personal life was becoming more complicated. In New York City, she and Cressman were able to see each other once or twice a week. He was now an apprentice minister and a graduate student in sociology at Columbia; their marriage was pending. However, Mead's father opposed her marriage to Cressman, offering to support her graduate education as well as provide an additional sum of money if she terminated her engagement to him. Mead refused, and her father cut off her funding. Benedict provided Mead with three hundred dollars from her own funds, and sociologist William Fielding Ogburn offered her a paid position as a research and editorial assistant, allowing Mead to attend graduate school and marry Cressman.

After their five-year engagement and shortly after Mead graduated from Barnard, the couple married, spending their honeymoon on Cape Cod. However, despite all their reading and discussions about sex, and despite the liberal environment that their friends provided, they were still novices, and their wedding night was not quite what they had desired. Mead wrote that, after five years of engagement, there were "moments of strangeness and disappointment to overcome."

We had read so many books written by sex specialists of the 1920s who believed that sex was a matter of proper technique—that men should learn to play on women's bodies as if they were musical instruments, but without including in the calculations that women must be very good musical instruments in order to please the men who played on them. (Mead 1972: 126)

Cressman was more candid:

> We came to each other at marriage as virgins. Although quite sophisticated intellectually and verbally, we were both physically and emotionally immature. I, four years Margaret's senior and with much wider experience, was the more mature. During these early days of our honeymoon we both, I think, had a sense, an awareness we could not quite conceal that something expected, hoped for, was lacking. (Cressman 1988: 92–93)

On their honeymoon, the couple used separate bedrooms because Mead insisted that she had to prepare for a seminar. Cressman did not quite believe her and later wrote, "Margaret, as she so often did, was dramatizing a situation and, I think, seeking to avoid an experience and a possible emotional commitment she preferred not to have.... I am afraid we were both rather relieved when our days on the cape came to an end" (1988: 93).

Marriage was just one of Mead's personal commitments. As she pursued graduate work in anthropology, her personal relationships often involved other anthropologists. Sometime after Mead chose anthropology, she and Benedict became intimate, a dangerous liaison in the 1920s. Both Mead and Benedict knew that if their relationship was publicly exposed, it would cost them their reputations and careers. Both were married. There were not only sexual and intellectual dimensions to their relationship but a teacher-student dimension as well. Although the intimate aspect of their relationship ended in the late 1920s, Mead and Benedict remained close friends and inseparable intellectual companions until Benedict's death in 1948. The full nature of their relationship did not become public knowledge until 1984, sixty years after it began and several years after Mead's death.

Mead thought of her marriage to Cressman as a "student marriage," one that allowed each of them time to study without the distraction of looking for permanent companionship. But Mead had additional companionship from Benedict and other female friends. There was also Mead's relationship with Edward Sapir, a Boas protégé, brilliant linguist, and influential anthropologist.[1] Mead and Sapir met at a small professional meeting in Canada in 1924 and were immediately attracted to each other, although Sapir was seventeen years her senior and a widower with three children. They exchanged passionate letters and poetry, with Sapir writing to Mead: "Margaret, we must have a little child together someday. In or out of wedlock, I just feel the mystical necessity" (Blum 2017: 164). Sapir was so taken with Mead that he tried to persuade her to divorce Cressman and marry him (Darnell 1990: 184).

For his part, Cressman accepted Mead's interest in an open marriage with the understanding that other relationships were temporary and that their marriage came first. Committed to Mead, Cressman nevertheless sensed that these other relationships were becoming a factor in their marriage. He also recognized Mead's growing professional ambition and realized that her career goals as an anthropologist might eclipse their relationship. Their future was uncertain, even as Mead's future in anthropology was becoming clearer.

When Mead entered the PhD program in anthropology at Columbia, she did so as one of a very small number of students in the department. In the United States at that time, there were only two major graduate programs, very few professionally trained anthropologists, even fewer women anthropologists, a handful of positions in academia, little financial support, and a minimum of professional education by today's standards. Yet Mead was fortunate to be at Columbia because during the early decades of the twentieth century, the department was a major force in the young discipline, particularly in cultural anthropology (Eggan 1968: 133). Boas and his students were responsible, in part, for setting and implementing the discipline's research agenda. The Columbia department was also unusual in its support for women graduate students. Between 1914 and 1929, the department of awarded eighteen PhDs, of which ten were to women, including Mead.

In the Columbia department, there were few graduate courses and seminars, and only a limited anthropological literature to master. It took Mead a little more than a year after receiving her MA in psychology to complete her PhD dissertation in anthropology. In contrast, today a newly minted PhD in anthropology takes an average of over eight years after completing a bachelor's degree, partly due to the time-consuming nature of fieldwork in another culture.

THINKING ABOUT FIELDWORK

Mead did not engage in fieldwork for her dissertation. She wrote a library- and museum-based study of the distribution and stability of certain Polynesian cultural traits, including tattooing, canoe building, and house building (Mead [1928a] 1969). This kind of dissertation was not unusual at the time, but fieldwork was becoming the measure of professional credibility in cultural anthropology. Time spent in another culture doing ethnographic fieldwork was, and continues to be, considered the best way to learn about another culture. It was also a professional rite of passage.

While pursuing her graduate education, Mead attended professional meetings and listened to anthropologists talking about their fieldwork and their "people." Mead wanted a "people" of her own. She knew that as soon as she finished her dissertation she would go to the field. Cressman already had a scholarship to study in Europe for 1925–26, and the couple agreed that each of them needed a period of further professional training.

Since Mead had written her PhD dissertation using Polynesian material, she wanted to do fieldwork in that region of the world. She hoped to travel to the remote and exotic Tuamotu Islands in French Polynesia, but Boas was concerned about her personal safety. Prior to Mead, there had been only one American woman who conducted dissertation research outside the continental United States. Almost all of the new PhDs in the United States at that time were working with Native Americans.

If Mead insisted on fieldwork in Polynesia, Boas informed her that she would have to choose an island where a ship came at least once every few weeks. Mead agreed and chose American Samoa, a territory administered by the U.S. Navy. By chance, Cressman's father knew the surgeon general of the Navy, who agreed to have his staff in American Samoa keep an eye on Mead and assist her with contacts in the islands. Nevertheless, Boas, Sapir, and other colleagues were worried about her ability to survive in the field. Mead was small and seemingly frail, having broken an ankle in an accident as well as having painful neuritis in her arm.

In need of funding, Mead applied for and received a National Research Council fellowship to study adolescence in American Samoa. The definitive study of adolescence from that period was authored by psychologist G. Stanley Hall (1904), who reported that adolescence everywhere was a time of "storm and stress," anxiety, and rebellion. But was this finding really universal? Boas had suggested the general topic of adolescence to Mead because the cross-cultural study of how people learned their culture from birth to maturity was largely unexplored. And while he encouraged Mead to pursue this topic, there were no guidelines for this kind of research. How she chose to conduct the research was up to her. Before leaving for the islands, Mead met with Boas for about half an hour to get advice. Otherwise, what she knew about the experience of fieldwork was what she had gathered from informal conversations with friends and teachers; it could not have been very much.

With fieldwork approaching, Mead and Cressman were coming to a crossroads in their marriage. They had come a great distance from dreams they had shared when they became engaged. Mead was now fully immersed in an academic career and no longer thought of herself as being a minister's wife with the ambition of having several children. Her personal relationships with Benedict and Sapir were posing problems for her marriage. Cressman himself was questioning his dedication to becoming a minister and would soon abandon that career altogether to become a sociologist and, later, an archaeologist.

In the summer of 1925, Mead prepared herself for the long journey to the islands. Then she and Cressman took a last vacation together and said goodbye. They planned to meet again in France the following year. Mead made her way west, visiting Benedict in New Mexico. On the train, she wrote to Cressman about her relationship with Sapir in order to share with him what she had not been able to tell him in person. Then, just before departing from San Francisco to Hawaii by ship, Mead wrote Cressman another letter with a sentence stating "I'll not leave you unless I find someone I love more" (Freeman 1999: 66).

NOTES

Jane Howard's *Margaret Mead: A Life* (1984) is the best overall biography. Mead's autobiography of her early career (1972) and Mary Catherine Bateson's *With a Daughter's Eye* (1984), as well works by Lois Banner (2003) and Hilary Lapsley (1999), are important sources on her early career. Nancy Lutkehaus' book on Mead as a public figure (2009) is also recommended. Clifford Geertz's biographical essay (1989) provides an excellent summary of her life. An annotated bibliography of works by and about Mead is available (Shankman 2018a). Among the documentary films on her life, *Margaret Mead: Taking Note* (Peck 1981) is the best.

1. Regna Darnell's (1990) biography of Sapir is the essential study of Sapir's life and work.

CHAPTER 2

FIRST FIELDWORK IN SAMOA

● ● ●

Fieldwork for a young woman traveling abroad and working alone was not easy in the 1920s. Mead was only twenty-three and had never visited another culture prior to American Samoa. She had never been west of the Mississippi, let alone traveled beyond North America. She had not spent a day alone before her fieldwork began and had not spent a night in a hotel by herself. Her mentors worried that Mead might be setting herself up for failure. Sapir, hoping to marry her, tried to prevent Mead from leaving. He approached Boas and Benedict, expressing concern that her physical and mental health would be at great risk in the islands. Boas admitted that Mead could be "high strung and emotional" (Lapsley 1999: 121), but defended her as determined and capable. Benedict also supported Mead. She would eventually learn of Sapir's attempt to derail her fieldwork and would deeply resent his interference.

Mead prioritized fieldwork over domestic life, including a life with Sapir. She wanted to end their relationship but was unsure about how to initiate a breakup. Prior to leaving for the islands, Mead sought advice from Benedict, who had already learned about the affair from Sapir himself. Benedict was appalled. Sapir was her closest male friend, and Mead was her lover and advisee. In addition, Benedict had been attracted to Sapir. Learning about the Sapir-Mead relationship was traumatic for Benedict. After Mead informed her directly, the two women had an extended conversation about their future, making a pact to put their love for each other first. They then developed a strategy for ending

Sapir's hope of marrying Mead. In her letters, Mead would write Sapir of her interest in free love, a philosophy that he abhorred. Presumably Sapir would then reject her because she was not the traditional domestic partner and homemaker that he desired.

Traveling by ship to Hawaii, Mead stopped to meet with colleagues at the renowned Bishop Museum in Honolulu. There she agreed to conduct a general study of Samoan ethnology for the museum while also studying Samoan adolescence, funded by her fellowship from the National Research Council. In return, Mead received the title of associate in ethnology at the Bishop Museum and entered into an agreement to have her findings published in the museum's bulletin series. These were good career moves. After Honolulu, Mead continued her voyage by ship to American Samoa, about 2,500 miles to the southwest, arriving in the port of Pago Pago in late August 1925. Cressman's father's naval connections were there to assist her.

Apart from official recognition, Mead's presence in Pago Pago drew the attention of the American expatriate community. Her unconventional marriage, allowing her to be away from Cressman for long periods of time, did not go unnoticed. As a young woman alone, she became the object of local gossip. Nevertheless, Mead focused on her project. Naval officials provided her with a Samoan nurse to help her learn the language, and she began to study it almost immediately.

Mead was interested in Samoan culture, but American Samoa was not a pristine, untouched locale, nor had it been for some time. Samoans had become devout Christians decades earlier and were part of a cash economy. This group of islands was an American territory under the jurisdiction of the U.S. Navy. Pago Pago, the port town, had one of the best harbors in the South Pacific and was an important coaling station for naval ships. Navy personnel seemed to be everywhere. So American Samoa, with a population of about 20,000 Samoans, was not a hidden paradise awaiting discovery. It was a small tropical hub in a colonial empire. In this setting, relations between Samoans and the naval administration were strained. Samoan resistance to naval policies coalesced into an organized opposition.

CHOOSING A FIELD SITE

Mead was aware of these administrative problems, but she was
more concerned with finding a village where she could begin
her study of adolescents. The island of Tutuila, where she was
learning Samoan, was a logical place to look for a field site but,
after touring the island's numerous villages, Mead wondered if
she would find a suitable site there. In a letter to Boas, she wrote
that villages were either westernized because they were on the
bus line, or small and isolated. The westernized villages were of
no interest to Mead, while the small villages had only a handful
of adolescents each.

On the other hand, Ta'ū Island in the Manu'a group seemed
ideal. This group of islands was about 68 miles by boat to the east
of Tutuila, less westernized, and more culturally conservative.
The only Americans on Ta'ū were the Holt family, who ran the
naval medical dispensary, and two navy corpsmen. Mead wrote
to Boas:

> Ta'ū is the only island with villages where there are enough
> adolescents, which are at the same time primitive enough
> and where I can live with Americans. . . . In Ta'ū I will be
> living at the dispensary with the only white people on the
> island and right in the midst of the village. I can be in and
> out of the native homes from early in the morning until late
> at night and still have a bed to sleep on and wholesome food.
> The food will be much better than the hotel food [on Tutu-
> ila] because Navy people have canteen privileges. Mrs. Holt
> is a sweet woman, was a schoolteacher, and I think I shall
> enjoy living with them . . . . It is really optimum in every way
> because I will have infinitely better care than I could possi-
> bly have in one of the remote villages on Tutuila. (1977: 28)

Mead's rationale for doing fieldwork on Ta'ū had to do largely
with the sheer numbers of adolescents readily available, the
lesser effects of westernization on the villages of this island, and
the comforts of living with the Holts. Ta'ū provided a unique set-

ting in which several hundred Samoans lived in close proximity to each other in three different villages. While still on Tutuila, Mead realized that Ta'ū could yield a sample of several dozen adolescent girls.

"NERVE-WRACKING CONDITIONS"

Mead was also concerned about living with a Samoan family, believing that the "nerve-wracking conditions" in doing so would slow her fieldwork. Should she have been so concerned? Ideally cultural anthropologists are supposed to be "dirt fieldworkers," living with indigenous families, eating their food, speaking their language, enduring whatever inconveniences and hardships that may occur, and overcoming "culture shock." As a rite of passage, this process enables fledgling ethnographers to become authentic participant-observers who are not only knowledgeable about a culture but who become part of it. However, this ideal is often not fully realized. Like the fieldwork of so many of her contemporaries, Mead's immersion in Samoan culture was imperfect and sometimes difficult.

Mead's letters from the field reveal frustration, embarrassment, and illness. She was lonely, homesick, self-critical, and sometimes worried that she was not learning enough or acquiring enough good data to please Boas. The physical challenges of the islands were trying. The neuritis in her arm flared up, the mosquitoes were voracious, the cockroaches were as "big as mice" (Caffrey and Francis 2006: 11), and the heat and humidity were exhausting. Mead sometimes felt that she was going to fail. In a letter to Benedict, she declared, "I'm just going to give up and get a job taking change in a subway" (Banner 2003: 240).

Mead did try to anticipate her own limitations—for example, her concern about Samoan food. She candidly admitted, "I can eat native food, but I can't live on it for six months" (1977: 28). Indeed, it was not easy for her to adjust to the high-carbohydrate Samoan diet, at that time consisting mainly of taro, bananas, and breadfruit.

There were social challenges in living with Samoans as well as physical ones. Samoan families could be extremely hospitable, generous, and helpful. Mead's letters to Boas and her friends show her appreciation of the privileges of rank that she was given when she was appointed a ceremonial virgin, or *taupou*, of a chiefly family that she stayed with on Tutuila. Yet rank also had its drawbacks, restricting her contact with girls from families of lesser rank and preventing her from studying the general population of adolescent girls. This was another reason that Mead wanted to live with the Holts on Ta'ū.

Privacy was another consideration. As a single American woman, Mead could not live alone; the naval administration would not permit it. Wherever she resided, she would be the object of much curiosity, especially from Samoan children. If she lived with a Samoan family, even the most rudimentary Western conventions of privacy could not be taken for granted. Samoan families lived together in open-sided houses known as *fale*. There were no walls, doors, or windows. As a result, social life was very public, and Samoans viewed privacy as dangerous because they felt that people only sought privacy when they wished to do something that was socially unacceptable.

Mead became familiar with these problems—food, comfort, rank, and privacy—after spending ten days living in a chiefly household in the village of Vaitogi on Tutuila. This firsthand experience was largely pleasant, but there was an additional problem in Vaitogi and elsewhere on Tutuila. Mead was not only an honorary ceremonial virgin in the Samoan system of rank, she was also associated with the U.S. naval administration, and therefore was considered by Samoans to be a very important person. Her status in the colonial order made fieldwork with children and adolescents difficult; from a Samoan perspective, she was too important for that.

Mead tried to negotiate where and how to do her research, given these constraints and her own preferences. She wanted to maximize her research time with Samoans and thought that the Holt household would provide the best base of operations. Mead's concerns about comfort and company were not unrealistic, and they were secondary to her research goals. She did not choose Ta'ū for comfort's sake. Had Mead sought more familiar surroundings, she could have remained in Pago Pago, residing at the hotel where the British writer Somerset Maugham penned his famous short story "Rain." Yet Mead was eager to go to the remote Manu'a group and, while there, travel without naval escort. So, after two months of language training and exploration on the main island of Tutuila, she set off for Ta'ū and settled in with the Holts.

ADOLESCENT GIRLS

Mead used her room at the back of the Holt house to meet with Samoan girls individually and in small groups, as it was a very convenient place for visiting. The room opened onto a village. The girls enjoyed Mead's company and attention, visiting her in their spare time. At five foot two and a half inches and ninety-eight pounds, Mead was often smaller than they were. Samoan parents allowed their daughters to visit her because Mead associated herself with education, something they greatly valued. Mead also "borrowed" a schoolhouse and gave the girls psychological tests that she called "examinations," as well as talked with them one-on-one. By getting to know the girls individually, away from their homes and peer groups, she was able to obtain information that would not have been available in more public settings. Mead also preferred the casual give-and-take of unstructured conversations to more formal interviews.

Over a period of five months, Mead became a familiar part of the girls' lives. They addressed her informally as Makelita (Margaret in Samoan). They assumed that Mead was, like them, young and single; she concealed her marital status. Her perceived status as an unmarried young woman led to courtship by at least one young man. On another occasion, Mead received a marriage proposal from a high chief that she politely declined. Mead fit well into the role of a young woman of note, being appointed as an honorary *taupou* not once but on three separate

Figure 2.1. Margaret Mead and a Samoan friend, ca.1926, American Samoa. Courtesy of the Institute for Intercultural Studies, Inc., New York.

occasions. And she learned to perform Samoan dances. As Mead became a participant-observer, she felt that she was beginning to understand Samoan culture from the perspective of adolescent girls.

Although Mead spent much of her time with adolescents and women, she also spent time with men, including chiefs, because of her interest in social organization and her appointment as a *taupou*. While she could not attend some chiefly occasions because she was a woman and could not participate in village political life, she nevertheless conversed with chiefs and untitled men. And Mead combined her interests in adolescence and social organization, working on both topics at once when possible.

The kind of fieldwork Mead was doing in American Samoa was different from that of most cultural anthropologists working with Native Americans in the continental United States. Native Americans had been confined to reservations by the federal government. In most cases they had lost their land and, displaced and impoverished, were thought to be losing their culture. With little funding and little time for research, ethnographers working in North America drove to reservations for a few days, maybe a month, or perhaps a summer. Their task was to reconstruct precontact Native American culture, recovering the past before it was lost forever. This was, quite literally, "salvage anthropology"—or "memory ethnography," as it is sometimes known—with little time for immersion in the field or for learning indigenous languages as the spoken word. Working with older informants who might remember precontact indigenous life, these ethnographers often regarded contemporary reservation culture as "broken" and of less interest.

However, for Boas and his students, interest in historical reconstruction was giving way to an interest in how contemporary cultures were integrated wholes, requiring consideration of how a culture was learned and experienced by its members. It was becoming necessary to study individuals within their cultural context. This kind of research involved more intensive and more lengthy fieldwork of the kind Mead was doing in her work on adolescent girls. On Taʻū, she spent months immersing herself in a "living" culture, and she was grateful for this unique opportunity. Although American Samoa was a colony, Samoans were never defeated in war or displaced from their land; much of their culture was intact. As Mead would later reflect on Benedict's fieldwork among Native Americans, her mentor "never saw a whole primitive culture that was untroubled by boarding schools for the children, by missionaries and public health nurses, by Indian Service agents, and sentimental or exiled white people" (1959: 206).

LEARNING THE LANGUAGE

Mead was in American Samoa for a little over eight months altogether, not a long period of fieldwork by today's standards. How well could she have learned the Samoan language and understood their culture? According to Mead, she not only spoke with a wide variety of Samoans, she spoke with them in their own language. Mead had not studied Samoan in detail before she began her research. She did spend a week studying Samoan as well as two related Polynesian languages while at the Bishop Museum in Honolulu in transit to American Samoa. But she believed that it would take at least a year or more to learn Samoan well. Furthermore, she spent only eight weeks on Tutuila learning Samoan before traveling to the Manu'a group.

Mead did have training in linguistics that she received from Boas, and this facilitated her learning Samoan. Within three days of her arrival in American Samoa, she began learning the language with the aid of the Samoan nurse assigned to her for this purpose. She resolved to do no other work and to study the language eight hours a day. Adding to her study of standard Samoan, one chief took it upon himself to instruct Mead in the more specialized honorific language of chiefs during her ten-day stay in Vaitogi. Mead gradually became more confident in her language ability, and, after two months on Tutuila, was ready to move to the more remote Manu'a group.

While on Ta'ū, Mead not only continued to learn Samoan; she even became an interpreter for a U.S. Navy lieutenant commander. Mead acknowledged that there were three Samoans on Ta'ū who could speak better English than she could speak Samoan. Her translations for officials were checked by a Samoan interpreter and contained very few errors. In addition, Mead was called on to act as an interpreter in a court case involving a land dispute between chiefs. She was nervous, but was able to interpret nonetheless. And she acted as an interpreter in an emergency medical situation when Samoan nurses were not available. Thus, within a few months of arriving in American Samoa, Mead was reasonably competent in the language.

For Mead, learning Samoan was facilitated by the English-speaking abilities of Samoans, as there was a fair amount of English spoken in the Manu'a group even in the 1920s. The highest-ranking chief had been educated in Hawaii, and a number of

Samoans, including adolescents, spoke English with varying degrees of proficiency. Mead spoke English with them, thus mitigating her self-admitted limitations in Samoan during her early months of fieldwork. By February 1926, though, she felt proficient enough to go to the village of Fitiuta, where almost no English was spoken, and work without an interpreter.

As she learned the language, Mead learned more about adolescent girls through informal interactions with them. She worked long days, from dawn until well into the evening. She recalled, "The adolescent girls, and later the smaller girls whom I found that I also had to study, came and filled my screen-room day after day and night after night" (1972: 34). The girls visited her so often at the Holt residence that Mr. Holt became annoyed at their constant presence. Samoans of all ages and ranks visited Mead on her porch; she sometimes had to lock her door to keep adolescents out, yawning prodigiously to get rid of them by midnight. And her visitors sometimes discussed sex to such an extent that, in a letter to Benedict, Mead complained that all they wanted to talk about was "sex, sex, sex" (Banner 2003: 239).

While on Ta'ū, Mead pursued the strategy that she and Benedict had discussed for terminating her relationship with Sapir. In letters to him, she presented herself as a woman uninterested in monogamous relationships. Sapir wrote her a number of letters protesting Mead's apparent self-centeredness and her not-so-subtle rejection of him. His letters filled Mead with self-doubt; she was still fond of him and respected his considerable intelligence. She hoped that her rejection of his insistence on marriage would not entirely sever their bond. Coming from a more traditional background, Sapir could not understand why Mead was reluctant to become his wife. Offended, he informed her that he had fallen in love with another woman, whom he subsequently married. Deeply conflicted, Mead lit a bonfire and burned all of Sapir's correspondence. For his part, Sapir was embittered by the end of their relationship, and this would have personal and professional consequences for Mead over the next fifteen years of her life (Darnell 1990: 187).

FINISHING UP

Mead's window for fieldwork on Taʻū was narrow. Seven weeks after her arrival there, a major hurricane struck the Manuʻa group. Mead and the Holt family sought protection from the storm inside an empty cement water tank. Samoan homes and crops were severely damaged, and in subsequent months all families were engaged in rebuilding efforts. Famine relief was necessary, and most ceremonial activities were suspended. However, the Holt house and medical dispensary were not badly damaged, and their food supply remained intact. Despite the hurricane's devastation, Mead continued her work, forging ahead and completing her fieldwork in mid-April 1926. She then returned to Tutuila, where she happily revisited Vaitogi, her favorite Samoan village, from which she wrote, "Here they love me and I love them" (Caffrey and Francis 2006: 204). She departed from Pago Pago in early May of 1926.

Mead did not have to leave American Samoa at that moment. She could have spent more time in the field by applying for another year of research funding from the National Research Council. Yet she did not apply because, while in American Samoa, she received a cable offering her the position of assistant curator at the American Museum of Natural History beginning in the fall of 1926. It was an offer too good to refuse.

As improbable as it may have seemed at the outset, Mead's fieldwork in Samoa was successful. With minimal guidance, she not only worked through the challenges of her first fieldwork but overcame the doubts of her colleagues in anthropology and of the naval administrators in American Samoa. Mead was courageous, energetic, resourceful, and a very quick learner.

UNRESOLVED ISSUES

Mead's fieldwork had ended, but what would she do with her research? And what of the personal relationships that she had put on hold during her fieldwork? Her relationship with Sapir had ended, but her relationships with Cressman, Benedict, and others were about to resume. With her fieldwork completed, the unfinished business of Mead's personal life resurfaced. She had left Cressman uncertain about the future of their marriage and left Benedict anticipating a renewal of their relationship. She would soon reunite with both of them in France.

However, during her long shipboard journey to Marseille, Mead met and fell in love with someone new—Reo Fortune, a young, tall, and handsome New Zealander headed to Great Britain for graduate work in psychology.[1] Fortune was very intelligent and dynamic but from a poor rural background with little experience in the wider world. Adventurous and naïve, Fortune was unlike Cressman in many ways. On their several weeks-long voyage from Sydney to Marseille, Fortune and Mead enjoyed the deep academic conversations that she had missed while in the islands.

In Marseille, Cressman was waiting patiently on the dock for Mead's arrival. But she and Fortune were in such intense discussion that they did not realize the ship was already in port. As they walked together on the deck, they unexpectedly encountered Cressman who, of course, had no prior knowledge of Fortune. Mead was profoundly embarrassed and a bit ashamed. Remembering this reunion, she wrote, "This is one of the moments that I would take back and live differently, if I could. There are not many such moments, but that is one of them" (1972: 175).

Mead was at another pivotal juncture in her life. Although she and Fortune were very much in love, Mead initially chose to stay with Cressman because she wanted children and felt that Cressman would be a better father. And she reunited with Benedict as well. After returning to the United States from France, though, Mead learned that she had a tipped uterus and would therefore be unable to carry a child to term; her pregnancies would probably result in miscarriages. Mead did not tell Cressman, but this was the precipitating event in their divorce. When she learned that she could not have children, Mead chose to pursue more fieldwork, and ultimately marriage, with Fortune.

On Mead's advice, Fortune had switched from graduate work in psychology to graduate work in anthropology at the University of Cambridge. Mead visited Fortune in Berlin in 1927 and three days later wrote to Cressman that she wanted a divorce. Cressman graciously accepted the inevitable. They would eventually divorce in Mexico because divorce in the United States was difficult at that time, and a Mexican divorce was both easier and more discreet.

NOTE

1. On Fortune's life and work, see Thomas (2009) and Dobrin and Bashkow (2006, 2010a, and 2010b).

CHAPTER 3

WRITING *COMING OF AGE IN SAMOA*

* * *

E ven as Mead worked through her personal relationships, she
began working up her Samoan field material. One of her first
obligations on returning from the islands was to write up her data
as a scientific report for the National Research Council, one of
the two institutions that sponsored her research. Under the su-
pervision of Boas, she set about writing an ethnography of Samoan adolescence. At the time, there were no models for writing
up the results of this kind of field study. So Mead pioneered the
ethnographic study of adolescence in a report drily titled "The
Adolescent Girl in Samoa" (1927a). The report was just that and
might have remained an obscure and uncontroversial document.
Yet within a short time it became *Coming of Age in Samoa*—her
first book, her best-known book, and her biggest seller. By the
time of Mead's death, it had gone through six editions, been trans-
lated into sixteen languages, and sold hundreds of thousands of
copies. The book is still in print today, nine decades after it was
written. How did the transformation from professional report to
popular bestseller take place?

While she was in Samoa, the *New York Sun* ran a mildly sen-
sational story about Mead as a "scientist" studying a different
kind of adolescence in a South Seas "jungle." The very fact that a
young "white" female anthropologist would venture into "primitive" Samoa to study untamed youth was news. Boas and his

colleague Clark Wissler sensed that Mead could use the public's fascination with distant Polynesia to provide Columbia and the American Museum of Natural History, Mead's new employer, with some popular attention. Mead understood this, too. She did not need prodding by Boas or Wissler. Deciding to turn her report into a popular book, she asked the National Research Council for permission to do so, and the council approved her decision.

Mead thought that she knew how to write for a popular audience. She had conscientiously honed her writing skills as a schoolgirl, aware that good writing was a valuable skill. Mead authored poems, essays, and plays during her school years, and continued to do so in college. As a graduate student, she worked with sociologist William Ogburn as an editorial assistant for a major professional journal. Mead also read books with a critical eye to their writing style and targeted audience. At Columbia, she read Boas's popular book, *The Mind of Primitive Man* (1911), but thought it lacked "the literary persuasiveness which its importance and its subject matter deserved"; Mead also knew that within anthropology there were writers, such as Sir James Frazer in England, who did not write in the "heavy German style that had captured the American university dissertation field" (Gordan 1976: 2–3). Thus, she consciously brought a literary approach to her writing.

Yet Mead did not have a track record of publications, popular or academic, before *Coming of Age in Samoa*. Her PhD dissertation was the longest piece of writing that she had completed prior to her report for the National Research Council. When published by Columbia University Press in 1928, the dissertation was only eighty-nine typeset pages in length. To turn her scientific report on adolescence on a remote island into a book, Mead would need a publisher willing to take a chance on an unknown female author from a relatively obscure discipline. Her report would need revision to appeal to a commercial audience, and it would need promotion to attract a substantial readership. The odds of all of these things happening were slim.

FROM SCIENTIFIC REPORT TO POPULAR BOOK

To help her revise her professional report for commercial publication, Mead sought the advice of George Dorsey, an anthropologist who himself had become a popular author. Dorsey advised her to submit the report to Harper and Brothers, a well-established publisher, but they rejected it. Mead and Dorsey then contacted William Morrow, a young publisher who saw how the report might find a wider audience if Mead added an introduction and concluding chapters to make it more relevant to the general public, and if she placed some of the methodological and historical material from the report in appendices. Mead and Morrow also discussed spicing up the manuscript, and she was willing to take his advice.

In the process of writing *Coming of Age*, Mead knew that some of her statements in the book manuscript were, frankly, speculative. In her correspondence with Morrow, she worried that she might be going too far in the text. In a letter to him, Mead noted that the last two chapters pushed "the limit of permissibility" (Côté 2005: 64). Morrow agreed that she might pay a price with her colleagues for popularizing her work, but they were both willing to take that risk. In rewriting her report as a popular book, Mead did not see herself as dumbing down her prose to the lowest common denominator. She simply wanted to make anthropology accessible to a broader audience. At best, her research report to the NRC might reach a few dozen professionals. A trade book could mean an audience of thousands of interested readers, perhaps more.

SAMOA IN PRINT

Mead wrote in what she called "literate English," a style later dubbed the "wind rustling in the palm trees" school of ethnographic writing, and for good reason. Passages in *Coming of Age* evoked images of paradise. In her chapter "A Day in Samoa,"

Mead wrote in a gentle, lyrical, and idyllic manner, offering sentences like this:

> As the dawn begins to fall among the soft brown roofs and the slender palm trees stand out against the colourless, gleaming sea, lovers slip home from trysts beneath the palm trees or in the shadow of beached canoes, that light may find each sleeper in his appointed place. ([1928b] 1973: 14)

The cover of the first edition of *Coming of Age* reiterated this theme, showing a young couple, both bare from the waist up, holding hands and anticipating a rendezvous under the swaying palms.

The structure of the book followed the Samoan life cycle from childhood through adulthood. After the introduction and "A Day in Samoa," Mead described in some detail the many facets of coming of age: child socialization, the Samoan household, the girl in her community, the role of dance, formal sex relations, personality, individuality, conflict, maturity, and old age. She found that Samoan children learned the "facts of life" early on, witnessing births, deaths, and, surreptitiously, even sex. Because Samoans lived in large extended families that often had more than one household, if problems arose, young people could move to a different household, reducing conflict. Furthermore, parents weren't necessarily primary caregivers; older female siblings were. Same-sex sexual activities were accepted for young children, although they were expected to be outgrown. During the years before marriage, girls could privately make choices about sexual relationships. Thus, in their transition to adulthood, Samoan adolescent girls experienced little rebellion or "storm and stress"; they were still far removed from the rivalries and strictures of adult life.

The chapters in *Coming of Age in Samoa* were full of interesting anecdotes about the people that Mead knew and studied. She incorporated individual stories into her topical coverage in ways that earlier anthropological works had not. What Mead tried to give readers was a sense of the actual lives of Samoan adolescents rather than an impersonal narrative about a distant culture. In the last two chapters, she drew explicit comparisons between Samoa and America because she wanted her book to be relevant to public concerns.

Mead offered Samoa as a mirror into which Americans could look for alternatives to their own culture, where adolescence was more difficult. She did not neglect rape, conflict, sexual restrictiveness, and aggression in Samoa, but she did downplay their significance. There are numerous examples of rivalry, competition, jealousy, and conflict in *Coming of Age in Samoa*. Indeed, there is an entire chapter titled "The Girl in Conflict." Yet Mead's interpretation of their place in Samoan culture gave them less emphasis and fewer negative connotations.

MEAD'S POINT OF VIEW

Like Boas, Sapir, and Benedict, Mead saw herself as a citizen-scientist. Not content with being a bookish academic, she wanted to be a public intellectual and activist, using ethnographic data to address important public issues. Although other anthropologists had waded into public debates periodically, Mead's primary goal in *Coming of Age in Samoa* was to reach a large segment of educated Americans on a subject of concern to them.

Most anthropologists of her era did not write the way Mead did. She was unequivocal and unafraid to offer her own opinions. Mead did not qualify or hesitate; she did not use words like *perhaps* or *probably*. Her use of dramatic phrasing suggested just how progressive Samoan adolescent girls were compared to American girls. She stated that they enjoyed premarital freedom, could experiment "freely," and had "many lovers for as long as possible" before marriage ([1928b] 1973:157,160,195). These phrases added a dash of excitement to Mead's staid professional report. Yet what may have seemed tantalizingly provocative to the American public in the late 1920s seemed truly problematic to some academics and popular reviewers at the time. The discontinuity between careful description and what Mead herself called the "almost drastic character of the conclusions" was evident even then ([1928b] 1973: 261).

Mead's views about sex, as expressed in *Coming of Age in Samoa*, derived from her experiences in young adulthood, including her interactions with her Barnard classmates, as well as Cressman, Benedict, Sapir, and Fortune. From her own experiences in the United States, the views of her social circle in New York, and the perspective that she developed there, she wrote that adolescence in Samoa was less stressful than in America. Samoan adolescents might have sex with less commitment, with more than one partner, and with partners of more than one gender. Mead herself knew what this might be like. Her discussions of the absence of romantic love and violent jealousy in Samoa also reflected her own views. She noted in a private letter that her Samoan adolescent girls seemed remarkably "modern" (Banner 2003: 243).

For Mead, *Coming of Age in Samoa* was not another ethnography in the short queue of monographs on other cultures that was developing in the early twentieth century. It was the first book by an American anthropologist to use ethnographic data from another culture as the basis for social criticism of American society. Mead went beyond simply describing and analyzing Samoan adolescence, as she would have in a standard ethnography and as she did in her report to the National Research Council. She was no longer a dispassionate ethnographer writing from "the native point of view" or from a purely scientific point of view. Mead was a moralist, writing from *her* point of view to an audience of American social workers, teachers, and parents.

Mead left little doubt about her own views of the personal lives of Samoan and American adolescents:

> From the Samoans' complete knowledge of sex, its possibilities and rewards, they are able to count its true value. . . . The Samoan girl who shrugs her shoulder over the excellent technique of some young Lothario is nearer to the recognition of sex as an impersonal force without any intrinsic value than is the sheltered American girl who falls in love with the first man that kisses her. ([1928b] 1973: 222)

The opportunity to experiment freely, the complete familiarity with sex and the absence of very violent preferences
make her experiences less charged with the possibility of
conflict than they are in a more rigid and self-conscious civ-
ilization. ([1928b] 1973: 160)

Mead was not writing as a cultural relativist in these passages.
Cultural relativism as an ethnographic tool assumes that other
cultures are worthy of study and that the ethnographer's own
moral judgments should be temporarily suspended so that cultures can be studied on their own terms. Although cultural relativism requires the temporary suspension of moral judgment and
comparison, it does not call for permanent suspension. Mead
practiced cultural relativism in her fieldwork and professional
work on Samoa, but in writing her book she made judgments and
comparisons that were very much her own.

Writing as a social critic, Mead reiterated that other cultures
might teach us something about America:

Realising that our own ways are not humanly inevitable nor
God-ordained, but the fruit of a long and turbulent history,
we may well examine in turn all of our institutions, thrown
into strong relief against the history of all other civilisa-
tions, and weighing them in the balance, be not afraid to
find them wanting. ([1928b] 1973: 23)

In this sense, *Coming of Age in Samoa* was utopian. Mead hoped
that American adolescence could become less stressful for adolescents and parents alike. Mead viewed Samoa as a kind of utopia,
and, in her interpretation, she minimized its less pleasant aspects
while emphasizing its more positive ones. Writing about the lives
of young women in a positive manner, she was also considered an
early feminist. There was no hidden agenda in the book, and her
direct approach connected with her readership. Mead also knew
that Samoa was not a realistic alternative for Americans. Americans could not become Samoans, but they might learn something
about themselves from Samoans nevertheless.

PRAISE AND CRITICISM

Working with her publisher, Mead quickly rewrote her scientific report. And, when the book was published in August 1928, William Morrow invested a substantial sum to advertise *Coming of Age in Samoa*. This helped to generate exceptional press coverage for the book. Morrow had also lined up strong endorsements from Dorsey, sexologist Havelock Ellis, and psychologist John B. Watson; their accolades were a major public relations coup and drew attention to the book.

One of the endorsements came from Bronislaw Malinowski, whose fieldwork in the Trobriand Islands set the standard for modern ethnographic work. In commentary appearing on the book's cover, Malinowski lavishly praised Mead's work, endorsing it as an

> absolutely first-rate piece of descriptive anthropology and an excellent sociological comparison of primitive and modern conditions in some of the most problematic phases of human culture. . . . Miss Mead's fieldwork seems beyond cavil or criticism. Her style is fascinating as well as exact and the book provides excellent reading; convincing to the specialist, attractive to the layman . . . an outstanding achievement.

Malinowski also wrote Mead personally to express his admiration for *Coming of Age*.

Following its release, tabloid-like headlines appeared in newspapers and magazines heralding the distant islands that Mead evoked in her book. They declared that "Samoa Is the Place for Women" and that Samoa is "Where Neuroses Cease." The praise Mead's book received was often unqualified.

Yet while many early reviews were positive, a number called attention to the inconsistency between Mead's description of Samoan adolescence and the generalizations that she drew from it. Among the most damning comments came from Sapir, Mead's former lover, who wrote in the *American Mercury* that *Coming of*

Age was "cheap and dull." In addition, he deplored feminists and lesbians, who he believed were both "frigid" and ambitious, and accused "emancipated women" of being little better than prostitutes (Sapir 1929a). In a private letter to Benedict, Sapir further berated Mead as a "loathsome bitch" (Banner 2004: 24). Having turned against Mead, Sapir attempted to persuade Malinowski to also do so, and Sapir's influence among a number of American anthropologists may have encouraged their negative views of her work. Anthropology was still a very small discipline, and Sapir was a major figure in it.

Professional criticism of *Coming of Age* would follow Mead for the rest of her career and after, coming both from those who knew her well and those who did not. In the 1960s, anthropologist Marvin Harris took Mead to task in his comprehensive history of the discipline, *The Rise of Anthropological Theory* (1968). Harris, who knew Mead while he was a student at Columbia and later as a faculty member there, agreed that Mead was one of "anthropology's most creative and brilliant personalities." Yet her "sweeping ethnographic generalities . . . leave many of her colleagues in a state of wide-eyed wonder." He cited as an example Mead's statement that "the [Samoan] girls' minds were perplexed by no conflicts, troubled by no philosophical queries, beset by no remote ambitions," commenting that, "for a generalization which is at once so sweeping and so thoroughly dependent on 'getting inside of heads,' Mead's style conveys an unnerving degree of conviction" (Harris 1968: 410–411). Like many other critics, Harris found that Mead "exaggerated."

Despite its commercial success, then, criticism of *Coming of Age in Samoa* came from many quarters. Some questioned Mead's data and conclusions, while others questioned her judgment. As Maureen Molloy observed in her analysis of Mead's writing,

> Her conflation of the modes of science, literature, and journalism was a reason for both her popular success and the ambivalence and hostility with which many of her professional colleagues regarded her work. The quality of her prose aroused suspicion if not wrath in the hearts of her fel-

low anthropologists, who are reported to have commented on her status as a "novelist" or "artist" rather than a "scientist." (2008: 6)

SOCIAL ORGANIZATION OF MANU'A

Coming of Age in Samoa was so influential that it has long overshadowed Mead's professional ethnography of Samoa. Less than two years after returning from the islands, Mead completed not only her professional report to the National Research Council and *Coming of Age in Samoa*, but also *Social Organization of Manu'a* (1930a), a major ethnographic monograph. Yet *Social Organization of Manu'a*, which received very little attention even within anthropology, was her genuine ethnography of the islands. Mead herself regarded it as her most important professional work on Samoa.

This monograph was written for anthropologists, contained almost no social commentary or cultural criticism, no utopian vision, and was published in the obscure Bernice P. Bishop Museum series where it languished in the shadow of its bestselling counterpart. The two books stood in stark contrast to each other. *Coming of Age* was a popular trade book about adolescence; it bore little resemblance to the ethnographies of that era. *Social Organization of Manu'a*, on the other hand, was a professional monograph on a decidedly unsexy topic. *Coming of Age* was boldly comparative; *Social Organization of Manu'a* was sober, cautious, and far more scholarly, building on earlier descriptions of the islands. Had this been the only book that she published on Samoa, Mead would have been remembered as a careful and pioneering ethnographer. And had she published it first, *Coming of Age in Samoa* might have had more professional credibility. Indeed, a number of Samoan specialists regard it as her best work on the islands. *Social Organization of Manu'a* is not flawless, but it is a very thoughtful study that was ahead of its time in terms of theoretical sophistication (Shankman 2005).

* * *

In these ways then, Mead's Samoan research launched her career and provided her with an understanding of the unwritten rules of fieldwork and publication. It also provided a guide for future field experiences that would consume much of the next decade of her life. Choose an unstudied culture. Select a topic of interest to the public as well as anthropologists. Obtain research funds. Settle in. Learn the language. Establish a comfort zone. Treat fieldwork as work. Write up the results quickly. Engage a trade publisher for popular work. Seek prestigious endorsements. Write a professional monograph later. Prepare for criticism. Repeat.

CHAPTER 4

MANUS AND THE OMAHA

● ● ●

Although Mead had wanted to author a popular book on Samoa, at the time *Coming of Age in Samoa* was published in 1928, the book's reception was of limited concern to her. She had not anticipated its success; neither had her publisher. Mead was not even in the United States when the book was released and reviewed. She was on her way across the Pacific to meet and marry Reo Fortune.

Fortune, now a graduate student in anthropology at Cambridge, had received a grant to work in New Guinea, and he asked Mead to join him. She was eager to do more research. With her position as assistant curator at the American Museum of Natural History secure, Mead had options for research that academic anthropologists in colleges and universities lacked. She did not have to teach on a regular basis and was not constrained by the academic calendar, so she could spend more time in the field than her academic counterparts. As a museum curator, Mead was responsible for representing cultures and collecting artifacts from the entire Pacific region. She was expected to travel and conduct research on behalf of the museum. In addition, there was an explicit public outreach dimension to her role as curator that allowed for communication with a broad audience, something in which her academic colleagues were less interested. Mead actively sought the role of public anthropologist, creating it largely through her own efforts.

As a scholar, Mead also wanted to contribute to the growing ethnographic record that was the bedrock of cultural anthropology. To improve the scope and quality of ethnography, Mead hoped to be part of a research team composed of both women and men to provide a more comprehensive account of the culture being studied and to avoid the personal and intellectual loneliness of doing fieldwork as a solitary ethnographer. She missed physical intimacy during her sojourn in Samoa and wanted this kind of companionship, as well as intellectual company, during her next field experience.

Mead was also becoming more interested in field methods and techniques. How could ethnographers produce more reliable accounts? For Mead, fieldwork was too important to be left to the idiosyncrasies of individual fieldworkers (1933). Preparation was vital because it enabled ethnographers to make the most of their time in the field, as well as producing better ethnographies. Since there were relatively few ethnographers at the time, and because the cultures they studied were rapidly changing, if not "vanishing," there might be only a single ethnographic account of a particular culture.

Mead felt that the best fieldwork not only required teams of men and women, but better documented observation, more carefully curated fieldnotes, and the use of psychological tests like the Rorschach ("inkblot") test that could be employed comparatively. She also thought that ethnographers had to become more self-aware of the nature of their interactions with the people they studied, calling for "disciplined subjectivity" or what is known as "reflexivity" today.

Although Mead emphasized the importance of doing research among unstudied cultures in her rationale for future fieldwork, her private relationships and professional connections played a major role in her selection of field sites and in her understanding of these cultures. This had been true for Samoa, and it would be true during her years in New Guinea. In Melanesia, two husbands—Fortune and later Gregory Bateson—would be her research partners, for better or worse, and Ruth Benedict would continue to provide her with intellectual inspiration.

MANUS

Crossing the Pacific by ship in 1928, Mead met Fortune in Auckland, where they married and laid out their research agenda.

Having left psychology for anthropology, Fortune was now going to conduct ethnographic fieldwork in the Admiralty Islands, a group not too distant from the Trobriand Islands made famous by Malinowski. Mead also secured research funding, this time to study childhood. Fortune had chosen Pere village on Manus in the Admiralties because it was unstudied and because he had met a young man from the village who would act as language instructor and translator. Traveling through Sydney on the way to Manus, Mead and Fortune met with Fortune's academic advisor, the influential anthropologist A. R. Radcliffe-Brown, for further preparation. Fortune, although still a graduate student, had already done fieldwork on the island of Dobu off the New Guinea coast. Thus, like Mead, he was an experienced fieldworker.

Australia had a multilayered administration in its colonial territories, including the Admiralties. Before entering Pere itself, Mead and Fortune met with the local government anthropologist and then with European residents, including shopkeepers and plantation owners. Now under Australian rule, the people of the region had previously been subjected to "blackbirding," a form of slavery in which indigenous Melanesians were forcibly taken to work on European plantations. Although blackbirding had been abolished, in Mead's time young men were still exploited as laborers, working for periods of two to three years on European plantations, on boats, or for the colonial police. They would then return to their villages with the money they earned to be used for arranging their marriages. Most of young men from Pere had worked on these plantations or elsewhere. So Pere, while unstudied and not yet missionized, was hardly untouched.

The village had a population of 210 people located about a quarter of a mile into a lagoon. The people of Pere constructed their thatched-roof houses on stilts over the water. Travel was by canoe—a "primitive Venice" in Mead's words. Even children aged three and four had their own small canoes. As a sea-dwelling people, the villagers made their living by fishing and trading with other island communities. There were forty-five households in Pere, erected fairly close together.

Mead and Fortune set up their new home in a comfortable government guest house reserved for visiting officials, employing several young people as cooks, laundresses, and research help. Mead was impressed by the quality of the food and immediately began to enjoy the culture where she and Fortune would spend the next six months. Mead believed that it was "the best field trip we ever had" (1972: 183), despite the couple contracting malaria. Malarial episodes reduced Mead's actual fieldwork time by a third; she also broke her ankle for a second time. Yet she was undeterred and continued to gather data.

Mead had looked forward to working with Fortune in the field. Although their research topics were very different, they could share experiences and improve their language skills together. In American Samoa, Mead's work on adolescence had led her to also examine the lives of children. In Pere, she wanted to explore how infants grew into adults. To what extent did a child's biology explain the transformation from infancy to adulthood, and to what extent was this transformation dependent on culture—mothers, fathers, siblings, and the learned environment?

The people of Pere were very different from the Samoans she had studied only three years earlier. Unlike Samoans, who were devout Christians, the people of Pere had not been missionized or provided with Western education. They lived in a world populated by ancestral spirits and ghosts who governed their lives. Mead characterized them as a puritanical, materialistic people "driven by ghostly mentors who punished them for the slightest sexual misdemeanor, like accidentally brushing against a member of the opposite sex . . . or when two women were heard talking about the husbands" (1972: 185). Bitter rivalries between families and individuals were thought to reflect conflicts among ancestral spirits.

Another difference between Samoans and the people of Pere involved gender roles. In Manus, fathers played a key role in the socialization of children as sympathetic guardians, while mothers played a secondary role in a child's affections. Mead carefully and systematically gathered information to understand how Pere children were being raised and by whom.

ANIMISM

Mead was also interested in certain Western theories about the development of children's thinking. In the early twentieth century, psychologist Jean Piaget believed that "primitive" people used "animistic" or supernatural thinking about spirits and ghosts that stood in sharp contrast to the rational and logical thinking that he attributed to Western adults. (The word "primitive" was part of anthropological discourse for much of the twentieth century.) Mead found that the adults of Pere clearly employed animistic thought, but what about the children? She decided to test the existence of animism among the "primitive" children of Pere.

Apart from spending a good deal of time interacting with the children themselves and observing them in play groups, Mead asked them to draw anything they liked; the drawings would be tools for understanding how they thought. For the first time in most of their lives, the children of Pere were given pencils and paper and asked to draw whatever they desired. Mead collected roughly thirty-five thousand drawings. If the children's mental worlds were dominated by the supernatural, the drawings would reflect an animistic universe of ghosts and spirits.

Instead, Mead found that the drawings were surprisingly realistic, indicating that their development was not characterized by animistic or irrational thinking. The boys' drawings often depicted fish, canoes, and humans. Girls' drawings were more colorful and used more designs. Thus, Mead found that, contrary to Piaget's ideas, there did not seem to be a stage of animistic thinking among Manus children; the presence or absence of animistic thinking was due to cultural factors rather than a universal "primitive" stage of social thought.

Mead wrote up her research results in a second popular book, *Growing Up in New Guinea: A Comparative Study of Primitive Education* (1930b), using a formula for exposition that she had employed in *Coming of Age in Samoa*. After describing in detail how children in Pere were socialized and after discussing their lack of animistic thinking, she devoted the second part of the book to a discussion of the relevance of Manus childhood for American children and their education.

COMPARING MANUS AND AMERICAN CHILDHOODS

Unlike Samoan children, Manus children did not experience an easy transition from childhood to adulthood. Their transition from childhood to the spirit-riddled world of adults in Pere was discontinuous and difficult. Moreover, Mead did not view Manus childhood positively, writing that Pere children

> have never learned to submit to any authority, to be in-fluenced by any adult except their beloved but not too re-spected fathers. In their enforced servitude to their older brothers and uncles, they find neither satisfaction or pride. They develop from overbearing, undisciplined children, into quarrelsome, overbearing adults who make the lagoon ring with their fits of rage. . . . They are never taught to re-spect age or wisdom. . . . They have learned no humility while they were younger; they have little dignity when they are older. ([1930b] 1960: 128)

Mead bluntly stated that childhood in Pere was not a "pretty picture" and, more worrisome, "in many ways, this picture is like our society today" ([1930b] 1960: 128). "We have seen how the Manus, like ourselves, give their children little to respect and so do not equip them to grow up graciously, how bringing up children to envy and despise their elders is doing those children scant service" ([1930b] 1960: 153). Mead thought that both Manus and American children needed better adult role models who could guide children into a more worthwhile adulthood, believing that American children should successfully participate in common experiences with adults rather than living separate and isolated childhoods like the children of Manus.

Advocating for the realization of human potentials, Mead in-sisted that children should be given "scope to the imagination"

([1930b]1960: 144) and should be brought up without regard to wealth and social position. According to Mead, this was not the case in Pere or America in the 1920s. She found dysfunctional behavior in Manus that she had not found in Samoa, drawing different lessons from each case. For Mead, Samoan childhood and adolescence were positive, even exemplary; childhood in Manus, like American childhood, was not.

With fieldwork concluding after six months, Mead and Fortune voyaged back to New York in September of 1929. Having left the United States before *Coming of Age in Samoa* was published, Mead returned as a well-known author, now in demand; her first book had become a bestseller. And Mead had accumulated $5000 in savings as a result of the book's sales, a considerable sum at that time. However, less than two months after their return, the stock market crashed and the Great Depression began. Although the crash did not initially affect Mead, her salary as a curator was reduced shortly thereafter.

Mead and Fortune found an apartment in the city and began transcribing their fieldnotes from Manus and writing up this material for publication. Fortune had transferred his graduate status from Cambridge to Columbia University and was also writing up his earlier material from Dobu, which was published as *Sorcerers of Dobu* (1932), an ethnographic classic. Mead quickly finished *Growing Up in New Guinea*. As with *Coming of Age in Samoa*, her publisher William Morrow sought influential reviewers whose comments could be used to publicize the book and boost its sales.

CRITICISM

Like its Samoan counterpart, *Growing Up in New Guinea* was mostly praised in the popular press and sold well. In 1930, anticipating further interest in her work, Mead hired a publicist to promote it. Yet professional reviews were mixed and some were quite negative. Had Mead spent enough time in the field? Could she have learned the language in six months? A. L. Kroeber, the distinguished head of the anthropology program at University of California at Berkeley, authored a lengthy and biting review (1931) in which he complained about the "paucity of ethnographic data" in *Growing Up in New Guinea*, unfavorably comparing Mead's work to Malinowski's. For Kroeber, Malinowski's ethnographic material was "unusually saturated, detailed, accurate, well integrated, and valuable," while Mead provided mere "scraps" (1931: 250). Even worse, he found that, in terms of theory, Mead's work "falls far below" that of Malinowski (1931: 249). And Kroeber wondered whether Fortune was going to provide information that her account lacked. For Kroeber, Mead was an "artist" rather than a scientist. Angered, Mead responded by writing him a long personal letter, politely but forcefully assuring him that she was a competent ethnographer rather than an artful dilettante.

This was not just a personal matter; senior anthropologists like Kroeber were the gatekeepers of professional reputations. Their reviews spoke to which kinds of studies were worthy of attention, whose work was important, and where colleagues ranked in the disciplinary pecking order. Mead's concern about such harsh reviews was warranted. In the small and predominantly male world of academic anthropology, her work was encountering strong headwinds.

A second review of *Growing Up in New Guinea* in the British journal *Man* was even more scathing. C. W. M. Hart, a student of Malinowski, directly questioned whether Mead's topic of choice—childhood—was worthy of anthropological inquiry. He also wondered whether Mead was "an anthropologist at all," criticizing her for "oversimplification and unjustifiable dogmatism" (Hart 1932: 46). And he implied that Fortune was probably the more accomplished ethnographer in the Mead-Fortune partnership. The negative tone of this review was apparently prompted by Malinowski, who had conveyed to Hart that Mead knew nothing about Manus kinship or their language (Mead 1976: 5). Mead was surprised and upset by this dismissal of her knowledge of Manus because she had been corresponding with Malinowski, and because he had just given *Coming of Age in Samoa* a superlative review. Challenged by Hart's review and wishing to demon-

strate her knowledge of Manus kinship to Malinowski, Mead
decided to postpone new fieldwork in order to write *Kinship in
the Admiralty Islands* (1934), a professional monograph reflected
her mastery of this complex subject.

A SUMMER ON THE OMAHA RESERVATION

As the Great Depression deepened, Mead and Fortune thought
about further fieldwork on the New Guinea mainland. Yet Mead
was also interested in doing fieldwork among Native Americans,
like so many of her colleagues who had been trained by Boas. By
coincidence, museum funds became available for a study of contemporary family life, including women's roles, among a Native
American group; Mead applied for and received them. Separately,
Ruth Benedict found funds for Fortune to study the vision quest
on the Omaha reservation in rural Nebraska. So, in the summer
of 1930, the couple spent three months working with the Omaha.

Unlike the Samoans and the people of Pere who, in Mead's
view, were "living" cultures, the Omaha were a reservation culture, their past "fading" and the people "broken" (1965: xii). The
Omaha experience was a "devastating" one, according to Mead.
They had been a buffalo-hunting, Plains Indian people. But that
was generations ago; the buffalo were gone and warfare as well.
There was little left of the pre-European culture. On the reservation, few Omaha men worked, simply renting out the land they
had been allocated by the government to white tenants.

Children were sent away to schools for Native Americans, and
they often returned alienated from their culture. In her later memoir, Mead recalled that "drunkenness was rife. Broken homes,
neglected children, and general social disorganization were evident everywhere" (1972: 208). Because the situation was so de-
pressing, Mead did not identify the group by name, but rather
used a pseudonym—"the Antlers." These people had been proud
of their culture; at the same time, the reservation was a place of
"disintegration, demoralization, and despair" (1965: xx). Only in

the 1960s did Mead use the actual name of the group in a reissue of her work there.

During the time she spent with the Omaha, Mead did not tell the people that she was an anthropologist (1965: xxi–xxii); in her words, she simply accompanied Fortune as a spouse with a "gossipy curiosity." She rationalized this "disguise" by stating that it allowed her to acquire material that she would not have been able to gather had she been open about her research goals and asked for their explicit permission to conduct interviews. In the 1965 edition of her book, *The Changing Culture of an Indian Tribe* (1932), Mead acknowledged that this kind of "disguise"—without the informed consent of the people being studied—would violate contemporary ethical guidelines.

Fieldwork in the summer of 1930 was "strenuous" and "grueling"; the sprawling reservation was hot, dry, and covered with dirt roads that connected the widely dispersed homes. There was no village, no cluster of centralized residences. The Omaha had been previously studied by other anthropologists, so the people were familiar with what the visiting couple might want and what they could extract from them. As a consequence of this familiarity, Mead and Fortune were viewed as potential sources of income, required to provide compensation upfront for interviews. "Indian English" was the language for most of the Omaha, so learning the indigenous language was not a priority as it had been during their earlier fieldwork in Samoa and Manus. Interpreters were used only for conversations with elders.

This was not the kind of fieldwork that Mead and Fortune foresaw. Writing to Benedict, Mead complained:

This is a very discouraging job, ethnologically speaking. You find a man whose father or uncle had a vision. You go to see him four times, driving eight or ten miles with an interpreter. The first time he isn't home, the second time he's drunk, the next time his wife's sick, and the fourth time, on the advice of the interpreter, you start the interview with a $5 bill, for which he offers thanks to Wakanda [the Great

Spirit], prays to Wakanda to give *him* a long life, and pro-
ceeds to lie steadily for four hours. (1977: 96)

Nevertheless, Mead was able to gather substantial data on families, women, and change. This was a different kind of research
for her. Mead was not simply collecting ethnographic data or re-
searching a generic topic like adolescence or childhood. She was
trying to understand how the transition from pre-European tribal
society to reservation culture altered the position of women
among the Omaha; it was not an encouraging picture.

Mead was quite explicit, observing that contemporary Omaha
women had virtually no role in the political, economic, and religious life of the group.

> The coming of white civilization found the position of Ant-
> ler women defined as follows: They were permitted no re-
> ligious privileges except such as they came through rank
> and inheritance, and these they simply held rather than ex-
> ercised; they were not trained for or expected to have any
> religious experiences; they played no public economic role
> beyond forming gift-exchange relationships with women
> from other tribes; they played no political role . . . they were
> expected to obey their parents' wishes in marriage and to
> conform to their husbands' preferences after marriage. At
> all times their behavior was to be meek, modest. They were
> expected to walk a few paces behind their men and never
> raise their eyes from the ground. (1965: 139–140)

Although in pre-European Omaha culture, women had some
status, contemporary Omaha women were often abused in marriage, and they sometimes left their husbands. Without male protection, though, these women were immediately vulnerable to
more abuse and rape. Mead provided detailed cases of the mis-
treatment of these women, obviously sympathetic to their plight.

In *The Changing Culture of an Indian Tribe*, Mead documented
the changes wrought by reservation life. However, unlike her
writing about Samoa and Pere, Mead did not author a popular

book on the Omaha. Consequently, her work among these people is the least known of the several cultures that she studied. And
in tone and substance it stands in marked contrast to her work on
other cultures.

With their difficult summer on the reservation ending, the
couple returned to New York. In early 1931, after writing up their
Omaha fieldwork and after Fortune received his PhD from Columbia, Mead and Fortune were intent on still more fieldwork.
She had now done fieldwork in three different cultures within
six years, authoring three books with another in the pipeline—an
impressive record for any ethnographer. And Mead was already
a sought-after public figure, featured in news stories and giving
public lectures as an intrepid woman adventurer who studied exotic cultures. She had not yet turned thirty.

CHAPTER 5

ARAPESH, MUNDUGUMOR, AND TCHAMBULI

* * *

Because she believed that she probably could not bear children, Mead continued to make fieldwork her mission. Mead and Fortune approached Boas about the possibility of studying the Navajo whose culture, unlike the Omaha, was "living" and "intact." Perhaps fieldwork among the Navajo would compensate for their disappointing experience among the Omaha. However, Boas informed them that the Navajo were already being studied and that the group "belonged" to other anthropologists. This was an era of ethnographic exclusivity when each ethnographer was expected to have his or her own "people." Since there was no shortage of cultures that needed to be studied, Boas encouraged the idea of "one culture, one ethnographer." Mead and Fortune would have to look elsewhere. For them, this meant a return to Melanesia, this time to the mainland of eastern New Guinea which, like the Admiralties, was under Australian rule.

THE MOUNTAIN ARAPESH

New Guinea was a huge island with more than eight hundred different language groups, steamy swamps, torrential rains, swollen rivers, dense forests, and an impenetrable mountainous interior. In the European imagination, the interior was thought to be particularly "wild." Indeed, the great high valleys of the New Guinea interior were not even explored until the 1930s, when gold was discovered there. Travel in the interior was often difficult. And living conditions were fraught with peril, including malaria and other diseases.

Mead wrote that, "New Guinea, along with the islands that surround it, was virtually terra incognita to Americans" (1968: vii). During the 1930s, she would study four different groups in this ethnographic frontier of cultures recently pacified and not yet missionized. With funding in hand, Mead and Fortune set off on the long journey by ship from New York through the Panama Canal and on to New Zealand, Australia, and finally mainland New Guinea itself. There was still no commercial trans-Pacific air travel at this time; just getting to the field took months. Communication was by letter and telegram.

In the interior of New Guinea, travel was by footpath. Mutually hostile tribes could easily prevent inland travel. Preparation for a trip into the interior required extensive planning and provisioning since there were few government guest houses and certainly no European trade stores and plantations. Mead and Fortune would have to bring all of their food, clothing, bedding, medicine, photographic equipment, and guns with them, as well as gifts and trade goods, like salt, matches, and razor blades, to pay for household help and ethnographic assistance. Apart these essentials, Mead's wardrobe included silver slippers, jewelry, a black velvet jacket, a camel hair coat, and silk underwear, although most of these items would undoubtedly remain in storage on the coast (Lapsley 1999: 209).

New Guinea would be more physically challenging than American Samoa, Manus, or the Omaha reservation. Mead and Fortune planned to reach and then study a group in the interior called the Abelam. At the government station near the coast, Fortune recruited roughly 250 indigenous porters to transport their gear through rugged terrain to the Abelam. Mead herself was carried in a hammock by six porters because she had re-injured her ankle, and this made walking impossible on the difficult trails. Then, quite suddenly, after three days of trekking, the porters abandoned Mead, Fortune, and all of their gear.

The couple could neither move forward to the Abelam nor return to the government station on the coast. They were stranded
in the village of Alitoa among a group of about two hundred people, whom they called the Mountain Arapesh. Alitoa was perched
on a narrow ridge. It was about a city block long and a dozen
yards wide, with bushy slopes jutting precipitously downward
for hundreds of feet on each side. Access to the thirty residences
in Alitoa was by "impossibly slippery paths."

Mead and Fortune settled in. They lived in a local house for
a week while having their own house built by villagers for the
equivalent of about ten dollars. The new house had a "big veranda, center room, store room and cook house" (Mead 1977:
104). On the veranda, they could enjoy "deck tennis," a game
played by tossing quoits. As on Manus, the couple hired young
"cookboys," "shootboys" (who shot pigs and pigeons), and additional household help.

In the mountains the weather was cool, and they were comfortable. And the food was good because a government official
had provided seeds to the people of Alitoa, who now grew pump-
kins, cucumbers, tomatoes, corn, and watermelons. As a result,
Mead and Fortune ate well. And they were not completely isolated. They were visited by the government anthropologist and
occasionally received mail from the coast. However, because of
her injured ankle, Mead was confined to the village. At the conclusion of their fieldwork, she had to be carried out by porters just
as she had been carried in. In contrast, Fortune traveled widely
in the region, leaving Mead alone for substantial periods of time.

The village was on trading routes between coastal Arapesh and
plains Arapesh groups, so people from elsewhere were often visitors to Alitoa and vice versa. The Arapesh were, in Mead's words,
an "importing culture" (1938). Although Mead and Fortune were
disappointed that they would not be able to study the Abelam,
a more populous group with large men's houses and elaborate
ceremonies, the people of Alitoa were pleasant and easy to work
with, according to Mead.

Mead's project in Alitoa was to examine the ways in which men
and women were expected to behave. To what extent were their

sex roles similar to or different from Western sex roles? (Mead did not use the term "gender," which came into common usage much later). Among the Arapesh, there was sex segregation complete with a separate men's house and sacred flutes that were taboo to women; according to Arapesh belief, viewing the flutes would have been fatal to women. There were also menstrual taboos. Otherwise, there were few ceremonials and little cultural elaboration. Mead and Fortune had hoped to witness something more dramatic, more eventful, than the "simple, impoverished" culture they encountered (Mead 1972: 212). Discouraged, Mead nonetheless practiced her language skills with Arapesh children, witnessed births, described their material culture, recorded texts, and administered Rorschach and other psychological tests, working from dawn to dusk.

Although there was a men's house and sacred flutes, for Mead the Arapesh seemed to lack the hypermasculine culture encountered elsewhere in New Guinea. She found that neither men nor women were aggressive; indeed, aggression and violence were actively discouraged. Both men and women were expected to be "cherishing, gentle people who anxiously responded to the needs of others" (Mead 1972: 214). Both were expected to raise and nurture their children. In other words, both Arapesh men and women took on gender roles that in America would be considered "feminine." According to Mead, their culture was mildly sexed. Men and women seemed to have roughly the same "temperament"—that is, the same general psychological configuration (1972: 217–218).

TEMPERAMENT

Benedict and Mead shared an interest in the idea of temperament, and it would become the central focus of Mead's research in New Guinea. Borrowing ideas from psychology and psychoanalysis, it seemed to them that temperamental differences applied not only to individuals but to groups of people and even whole cultures. Mead noted that men and women, while biologically different, might share temperamental similarities. Furthermore, culture clearly played an important role in shaping how individuals expressed inborn temperaments. Each culture might favor a certain temperament for a society as a whole or for a specific gender role. Thus, some cultures might be more aggressive, possessive, and competitive, while others, like the Arapesh, might be more caring, compassionate, and compliant.

As they were conducting fieldwork among the Arapesh, Mead and Fortune received a prepublication draft of Benedict's *Patterns of Culture* (1934), a book that would become anthropology's all-time bestseller. In it, Benedict spelled out her approach to cultures as configurations, an approach paralleling Mead's own thinking about temperament. For Benedict, cultures were not random collections of different traits or institutions haphazardly thrown together. They were coherent wholes with particular psychological patterns or configurations. As Benedict stated, "Any society selects some segment of the arc of possible human behaviors, and in so far as it achieves integration its institutions tend to further the expression of its selected segment and to inhibit opposite expressions" (1934: 254). Thus, "the significant sociological unit, from this point of view, therefore, is not the institution but the cultural configuration" (Benedict 1934: 244).

For Benedict and Mead, it was not the parts of a culture that determined the whole; rather, it was the configuration or temperament that influenced each part of the culture. Institutions like the family or economic system had to be understood in terms of the cultural configuration or collective temperament. And most individuals in a particular culture, although not all, would tend to conform to its particular configuration. Thus, for Mead, the Arapesh had to be understood in terms of the cooperative, nonaggressive character of the whole culture that in turn permeated its constituent institutions, such as the family, in which such nonaggressive behaviors were expressed. Concurrently, Arapesh families would socialize their children to be gentle, discouraging deviation from this norm. Finally, for Mead and Benedict, each of these configurations was unique, selected from the range of human potentials, and all were "equally valid patterns of life which mankind has created for itself from the raw materials of human existence" (Benedict 1934: 278).

Thinking about Arapesh culture in this way would prove productive for Mead, and she would continue to use temperament as an organizing principle in her other studies in New Guinea. Yet at the conclusion of her research among the Arapesh in 1931, she expressed regret, personally and professionally. Fortune agreed. Although fieldwork had been pleasant and productive, the Arapesh were simply not that interesting to these researchers; it was a "thin" culture, according to Mead. She and Fortune were interested in the analysis of events such as births, deaths, marriages, and ceremonials. The more events they observed, the more reliable their descriptions and interpretations. But with few such events among the Arapesh, Mead felt that she was not moving ahead theoretically. And because of her lack of mobility and subsequent loneliness as a result of her injured ankle, she had been depressed.

Although Mead may have wished for a more interesting culture, the professional work that she produced on the Arapesh was as extensive as any of the other seven cultures that she studied. In addition to a section of *Sex and Temperament in Three Primitive Societies* (1935), Mead published a series of five detailed monographs on the Arapesh, including an ethnography of their religion (1940). There is also a volume on a young Arapesh man, Unabelin, with whom Mead worked very closely. As she commented, "Unabelin was more than an informant. He was a friend whose temperament I found congenial and whose mind delighted me" (Mead 1968: ix). Mead recorded his stories and myths, and assessed his personality through the use of Rorschach tests.

Appearing in the Anthropological Papers of the American Museum of Natural History, these monographs are not well known or widely read, but they are a testament to Mead's commitment to basic ethnography. In them, Mead presented Arapesh data for future scholars to consider; theory could come later. Mead wanted to share her ethnographic work as soon as possible. Getting ethnographically dense information on the record before Arapesh culture was about to change was Mead's primary goal.

And change was right next door to the Arapesh, with one nearby group already heavily missionized and an oil company exploring in the area nearby.

THE MUNDUGUMOR

After eight months among the Arapesh, the relationship between Mead and Fortune was beginning to fray. They needed a break from fieldwork. But instead of returning to Australia or New York, Mead and Fortune made a brief visit to a coastal European plantation before entering the field once more, this time in the Sepik region. Believing that young anthropologists should spend most of their time in the field, this is what Mead wanted to do with her time. She had an almost bottomless appetite for fieldwork.

Mead insisted that the next culture that they study be truly untouched. Yet cultures along the great Sepik River were regularly serviced by small steam ships and government launches; the people were exposed to European trade and labor recruitment for European plantations, as well as to missionaries. Furthermore, some of these cultures were already considered the province of Gregory Bateson, a young British anthropologist whom Fortune knew from his time in Cambridge. Mead and Fortune did not want to tread on his turf. In these circumstances, the couple arbitrarily chose the first large unmissionized village off a main tributary to the Sepik. The people were called the Mundugumor (now known as the Biwat).

Mead wrote that "the Sepik stands for mosquitoes, crocodiles, cannibals and floating corpses—and I can assure you that we've seen them all" (1977: 130). The mosquitoes were everywhere; in preparation for their fieldwork, Fortune ordered a "mosquito room"—a structure nine by ten feet square to be assembled inside their house in order to keep the mosquitoes at bay while they worked. Otherwise, they were under constant attack.

Mead and Fortune actually had two houses built in the village, along with their usual crew of indigenous household assistants. Their move into the village was relatively easy. Being on a major tributary of the Sepik meant more access to European amenities. Furthermore, unlike the Arapesh language, the language of the Mundugumor was relatively easy to learn. And the people were easy to work with. She and Fortune could play more deck tennis before dinner.

However, Mead had serious reservations about Mundugumor culture. Warfare had been endemic in the area, and the Mundugumor were notoriously warlike. The Australian administration curtailed the practice by arresting and imprisoning two prominent Mundugumor leaders. While they had been pacified a few years before Mead and Fortune arrived, the people still had vivid memories of warfare and cannibalism. They were aggressive toward each other, and rivalries permeated the social landscape.

Another Mundugumor practice disturbed Mead on a more personal level. The "floating corpses" to which she referred were unwanted Mundugumor infants cast onto the river in bark sheaths. Down river these infants might be rescued from certain death by people from other groups, but in many cases the infants simply perished on the water, either by drowning or being eaten by crocodiles. Mead was so distressed by Mundugumor infanticide that she became more determined to have a child despite her miscarriages and her physician's certainty that she would not be able to carry a child through a full pregnancy.

For Mead, the Mundugumor were not a "good culture." In her autobiography, she candidly stated, "I loathed the Mundugumor culture with its endless aggressive rivalries, exploitation, and rejection of children" (1972: 224). Yet she recognized that the Mundugumor were experiencing major changes in their lives. They had not only been pacified, but village ceremonial life had come to an abrupt end. Most of the young men were away as plantation laborers. Like the Omaha, to Mead the Mundugumor seemed to be a "broken" culture.

Despite these circumstances, Mead was able to gather data on a number of topics, including the roles of men and women. By sheer coincidence, according to Mead, the Mundugumor presented a sharp contrast with the Arapesh in terms of "sex styles" or roles. She noted:

The Mundugumor contrasted with the Arapesh in every conceivable way. Fierce possessive men and women were the preferred type; warm and cherishing men and women were disallowed. . . . Both men and women were positively sexed and aggressive. In general, both rejected children, and where the children that were allowed to survive were concerned, adult men and women strongly favored children of the opposite sex. (Mead 1972: 223–224)

This striking contrast between the Arapesh and Mundugumor would become a key piece of Mead's argument about the nature of gender as articulated in *Sex and Temperament in Three Primitive Societies.*

Although she had collected important data during her fieldwork, Mead was frustrated by the mosquitoes, disturbed by Mundugumor infanticide and aggression, and upset by Fortune's neglect of her health. The sum of these experiences may be reflected in her relative lack of publications on the Mundugumor. Mead did not author a separate, stand-alone ethnography of this culture; nor did Fortune. Apart from their inclusion in a chapter in *Sex and Temperament*, Mead wrote little else about the Mundugumor. However, her fieldnotes, along with those of Fortune, were so thorough that anthropologist Nancy McDowell, who worked in the same region decades later, was able to use them in her ethnography of that culture (McDowell 1991).

THE TCHAMBULI

After three months among the Mundugumor, Mead and Fortune packed up their possessions and traveled by boat to the main government station on the Sepik, where they would spend Christmas with other Europeans. The saga of this part of their fieldwork in New Guinea has become the stuff of anthropological lore, chronicled in Charles King's (2019) nonfiction bestseller *Gods of the Upper Air* and reimagined in Lily King's (2014) award-winning novel *Euphoria*, as well as in popular and professional biographies of Mead. It is a tale of exhausting fieldwork in the Sepik lowlands coupled with a passionate love triangle involving Mead, Fortune, and Gregory Bateson. It was here that Mead's marriage to Fortune would unravel and a new personal and professional relationship with Bateson would begin.

After difficult fieldwork among the Mundugumor and during their long trip up the Sepik to the Christmas party, Mead and Fortune stopped to pick up Bateson, with whom they had been corresponding by letter. Mead had not met Bateson, and she was not in good shape psychologically or physically. She had lost weight, had another bout of malaria, and was depressed. When she was introduced to Bateson, he sympathetically observed, "You're tired" (Mead 1972: 227). For Mead, these were the first kind words that she had heard in months; her attraction to him was immediate.

Bateson was six foot four, charming, and three years younger than Mead.[1] He had done fieldwork in two other New Guinea–area cultures before working among the Iatmul on the Sepik. These early field experiences had been disappointing, and he yearned for anthropological companionship during his continuing research among the Iatmul. In the Sepik, Bateson, Mead, and Fortune struck up a fast friendship full of intellectual excitement and problematic interpersonal chemistry. On one occasion shortly after being introduced, Mead and Bateson stayed up for thirty straight hours talking about their work. Fortune was becoming uneasy about this new relationship.

In Bateson, Mead now had another field companion. Yet Bateson and Fortune were like night and day. Bateson came from a prominent upper-class British family that championed women's rights, was cosmopolitan, was quite comfortable with the ideology and practice of free love, and was bisexual. In many ways, he was the opposite of Fortune, who was from a poor, rural New Zealand family, believed in traditional male-female roles and sexual exclusivity, felt uncomfortable in the shadow of Mead's fame, and was jealous of Mead's interactions with Bateson. Fortune's occasional drinking and sometimes violent temper added to this potentially toxic cocktail of differing personalities.

Before arriving at the government station in Ambunti, Mead and Fortune had anticipated more fieldwork among an indigenous group in Australia. Bateson persuaded them to stay in the Sepik. He took them in his canoe with an outboard motor to one promising field site and then to the Tchambuli (now known as Chambri), where Mead and Fortune would settle in for four months of research. The Tchambuli resided on the shore of a beautiful lake, and Mead loved the location, with its pink and white lotuses floating on the water, and white osprey and blue herons nearby.

Bateson moved his own field site to a village not too far away. So these young and intellectually hungry researchers were able to interact in person and by local messenger service fairly often. Mead felt a new energy for fieldwork. She reflected, "I felt wonderfully released from prison—the prison of that Arapesh mountaintop, where I had been unable to step outside the village for seven and half months, and the nightmare prison of the disintegrating, hostile, and mosquito-ridden Mundugumor village" (1972: 229). Mead judged the working conditions among the Tchambuli to be the best since fieldwork on Manus.

The Tchambuli village was compact, containing about 550 people divided into three rival groups. It had elaborate men's houses and an active ceremonial life—features that Mead and Fortune had been hoping to find in their New Guinea research. There were so many interesting events happening—house building, canoe building, initiations, artistic endeavors—that the couple sometimes had difficulty keeping up with all of them. To supplement their own work, they selected local youths from each men's house to report to them on events of interest, paying them a razor blade for each report.

The couple had two houses built for themselves and immediately began learning yet another indigenous language. With Bateson's help, they began to understand where the Tchambuli fit into the local political landscape. Prior to the Europeans, the nearby and powerful Iatmul had waged war against the Tchambuli and driven them out of the area. It was only after pacification and with colonial support that they moved back to the lake and rebuilt their village. In fact, a number of Tchambuli spoke the Iatmul language, and, because Bateson already spoke it, he was able to facilitate communication for Mead and Fortune, making him a valuable partner in their work.

In her work, Mead continued to examine sex roles and temperament, just as she had done for the Arapesh and Mundugumor, conversing with Bateson and Fortune as they compared notes within the limited confines of the mosquito room in one of their houses. These conversations gradually led to what they believed was a major theoretical breakthrough. In Mead's words:

> As we talked, week after week, about Gregory's material and ours, a new formulation of the relationship between sex and temperament began to emerge. We asked ourselves: What if there were other kinds of innate differences—differences as important as those between the sexes, but that cut across sex lines? What if human beings, innately different at birth, could be shown to fit into systematically defined temperamental types, and what if there were male and female versions of these types? And what if a society— by the way in which children were reared, by the kinds of behavior that were rewarded and punished, and by its traditional depiction of heroes, heroines, villains, witches, sorcerers, and supernaturals—could place major emphasis on one type of temperament, as among the Arapesh and Mundugumor? And what if the expectations about male-female differences, so characteristic of Euro-American cultures could be reversed? (1972: 236)

This is exactly what Mead found as she spent time with Tchambuli men and women:

> Among the Tchambuli the expected relationships between men and women reversed those that are characteristic of our own culture. For it was the Tchambuli women who were brisk and hearty, who managed the business affairs of life, and who worked comfortably in large cooperative

groups. . . . Tchambuli is the only culture in which I have worked in which the small boys were not the most upcoming members of the community, with the most curiosity and the freest expression of intelligence. In Tchambuli it was the little girls who were bright and free . . . . Formally the men were in charge of their households, but in fact the women managed all the valuables. (1972: 234–235)

Thus, among the Tchambuli, as among the Arapesh and Mundugumor, the very definitions of what it meant to be a woman or a man were constructed by that particular culture rather than being universal or "natural." Mead had come to New Guinea to explore possible sex differences, but what she found were temperamental differences regardless of sex, raising the question of what "masculine" and "feminine" really meant. Mead and Bateson were so taken with these ideas that they applied to them the other cultures they had known, such as the Samoans and the Dobuans, as well as to individuals like Benedict and Sapir.

Mead and Bateson were also thinking about their own temperaments, finding them to be "close," compatible, and in marked contrast to Fortune's. Mead and Bateson were sensitive and maternal; Fortune was masculine and possessive. These discussions rapidly gave way to something more personal. As Mead confessed, "Gregory and I were falling in love" (1972: 237). For the sake of their fieldwork, Mead and Bateson knew that their emotions had to be kept in check. Nevertheless, the tension within this love triangle was mounting and was exacerbated by their close physical proximity in the claustrophobic mosquito room. Furthermore, all three of them had recurring bouts of malarial fever that could produce delirium and vivid hallucinations.

Mead was also pregnant, and, during one of their fights, Fortune, who was over a foot taller, struck Mead and knocked her down. She subsequently miscarried. Mead lashed out at Fortune, calling him a murderer, while Fortune accused Bateson of causing the miscarriage. Knowing that Fortune had a gun, Bateson hid it from him. The situation was escalating out of control. Whether or not the miscarriage was a result of the fight between Mead and

Fortune, it ended their relationship. And it contributed to the end of their New Guinea fieldwork.

Shortly thereafter, the three ethnographers assembled their gear, traveled down the Sepik, and returned to Australia. In Sydney, they soon went their separate ways. There, both Mead and Fortune found new relationships. They would not encounter each other in person for another two decades. Meanwhile, Bateson resumed an older relationship with a former female lover from his Sepik fieldwork.

Ruth Benedict, ever a major figure in Mead's life even at a distance, heard about all of this in Mead's letters to her. Mead confided,

> These last months have all the quality of near madness—sometimes great lucidity, sometimes ecstasy—often despair. Gregory and I full expected that the most possible outcome would be that Reo would shoot me, then Gregory, then himself—there was nothing we could do—except hold on patiently day to day. (Caffrey and Francis 2006: 84)

Benedict wrote back and encouraged Mead to not pursue a relationship with Bateson at that moment but rather to return to New York, play the role of deserted spouse, and ultimately divorce Fortune. Mead took this advice and, traveling alone, returned to New York. The larger issues in her marriage to Fortune—their different class backgrounds, his masculine persona and demand for sexual exclusivity, and her celebrity, especially when in New York—now seemed insurmountable. In addition, she worried about what her professional colleagues, especially Sapir and Malinowski, would think about the potentially scandalous situation that had developed in the Sepik.

While Mead was in the field, Sapir continued to disparage her, including her views on jealousy. In 1932, she responded in print to Sapir's argument that jealousy was proof of genuine love by stating that jealousy actually revealed self-doubt and an inferiority complex. Moreover, without mentioning Sapir by name, she questioned his masculinity, remarking that jealousy was a characteristic of men who were short, had weak sexual endowments, or were old. As historian Lois Banner observed, "It may not have been the wisest approach, given the loyalty of the men in anthropology to Sapir and his own dislike of her" (2003: 281).

THE "SQUARES"

Between the winter of 1928 and the spring of 1933, Mead spent most of her time either in the field—a total of about twenty-one months—or traveling to and from the field. On returning to New York in 1933, she would take a long break before her next fieldwork. Back home, Mead now had time to think about what she had learned in the field, to write up the results of her work among the Arapesh, Mundugumor, and Tchambuli, to polish her professional credentials among her colleagues in anthropology, to work on museum exhibits and collections, to renew old friendships and pursue new ones, to divorce Fortune, and to plan a future with Bateson. Bateson had returned to England, where he would finish *Naven* (1936), his classic work on an Iatmul ceremonial. Mead and Bateson corresponded often, with Mead sometimes writing daily. In their trans-Atlantic letters to each other, they prioritized their relationship; at the same time, they were open about other relationships in which they both were engaged.

Stemming from their work in the Sepik, Mead and Bateson continued to be interested in how cultures were integrated in terms of temperament, an approach they labeled the "squares."[2] During their conversations in the field, Mead, Bateson, and Fortune came up with systematic sets of contrasting temperamental qualities, such as aggression and competitiveness versus nurturing and caring, that could be applied cross-culturally. These temperamental profiles were similar to Benedict's dominant configurations.

Both Mead and Benedict emphasized psychological and emotional features as ways in which cultures were integrated. Yet they disagreed on some crucial points. Mead explicitly linked the "squares" to innate biology—that is, there was a limited palette of biologically given individual temperaments that cultures then sorted, either encouraging or discouraging particular types. Benedict did not employ this biological component; she based her configurations on broader cultural considerations such as religion and myth. There were problems with both approaches, but one problem with Mead's approach was determining exactly what was "innate" in particular individuals and precisely how such differences among individuals could be organized into a cohesive cultural pattern. This was not only an intellectual problem; it was also a political problem.

When Mead, Fortune, and Bateson left New Guinea, they had hoped to publish their ideas about the "squares" as a new and important way of thinking about cultural differences. Mead and Fortune had cabled Boas that they were bringing home "immensely important new theoretical points" (Mead 1972: 240). However, the world beyond New Guinea was changing in ways that they had not fully appreciated while they were deep in the Sepik. In early 1933, Adolf Hitler and the Nazi Party came to power in Germany on a platform championing the innate superiority of the so-called "Aryan race" and the equally innate inferiority of other so-called "races."

Mead and Bateson soon recognized that discussions of inborn differences were "politically loaded" because people "associate particular traits with sex or age or race, physique or skin color, or with membership in one or another society, and then make invidious comparisons based on such arbitrary associations" (Mead 1972: 240). They understood that Hitler's vision of the struggle for racial superiority would not result in the appreciation of cultural differences but rather in the potential annihilation of "inferior" peoples. Excited as they had been about the "squares," Mead now believed that a theory based on innate biological characteristics could be misinterpreted or misunderstood as akin to Hitler's ideas. As a result, Mead and Bateson postponed publishing work on the "squares." And with the outbreak of World War II in 1939, the "squares" were put on permanent hold, although their interest in temperament continued.

SEX AND TEMPERAMENT

Based on her New Guinea research, Mead wrote up her field material in her third popular book, *Sex and Temperament in Three Primitive Societies*, a comparative study of sex roles among the Arapesh, Mundugumor, and Tchambuli. She introduced the book with a disclaimer:

> This study is not concerned with whether there are or are not actual and universal sex differences between the sexes, either qualitative or quantitative. It is not concerned whether women are more variable than men . . . . It is not a treatise on the rights of women, nor an inquiry into the basis of feminism. It is, very simply, an account of how three primitive societies have grouped their social attitudes towards temperament around the very obvious facts of sex difference. (1935: 13–14)

Within a one-hundred-square-mile area in New Guinea, Mead had found three radically different permutations in sex roles. Among the Arapesh, both men and women behaved in a manner we would consider "feminine." Among the Mundugumor, both men and women behaved in a way that we would consider "masculine." And among the Tchambuli, roles were reversed with men conforming to the Western stereotype of women, and women conforming to the Western stereotype of men. These differences were startling to Mead and many Americans.

In the 1930s, America adhered to a single standard of masculinity and femininity. Mead's gender-bending study upended the idea that this standard was "normal" and universal. This was even more shocking to some Americans than Mead's earlier finding that adolescence was not necessarily a time of storm and stress and that sexual permissiveness prior to marriage was possible without social harm. Although *Sex and Temperament* did not have the immediate impact on popular culture that *Coming of Age in Samoa* had at the time, with the later development of the women's movement, the gay liberation movement, and the LGBTQ movement, as well as the advent of gender studies, *Sex and Temperament* drew more attention.

CRITICISM

There were problems with *Sex and Temperament*. Mead herself noted that it seemed like an incredible stroke of luck to have encountered three groups that supported her argument. Yet Mead did not choose these groups to fit her argument. An analysis of the chronology of her fieldwork makes it clear that her argument emerged from her fieldwork as it unfolded rather than being imposed on it from the outset. Nevertheless, some of Mead's ethnographically based interpretations were incorrect, overstated, or at least problematic, as was evident in the critical reviews of *Sex and Temperament* that appeared following its publication and thereafter.

Just as with criticism of *Coming of Age in Samoa* and *Growing Up in New Guinea*, reviewers faulted Mead for not spending more time in the field with the cultures she studied. Others subtly implied that her interest in sex roles was not "real" anthropology; rather, it was something that women anthropologists might research. And there was the familiar criticism that Mead's detailed descriptive material did not support the broad generalizations that she drew from her data. Richard Thurnwald, who had done fieldwork in New Guinea, provided one such review in the flagship journal *American Anthropologist* (1936). After an unusually long and exacting discussion of the internal contradictions in *Sex and Temperament*, Thurnwald concluded his review by praising Mead for contributing a "store of information" on women, sex, children, and education and offering "fascinating descriptions of daily life," and by noting that the book was "well-written and will recruit friends for anthropology" (1936: 667). But his professional assessment of her work was largely negative. Stung by this criticism, Mead (1937a) responded with a long and vigorous commentary in the same journal.

Mead was particularly worried about what Fortune might say about *Sex and Temperament*. Their estrangement was intellectual as well as personal, with Fortune no longer supporting the "squares" or their thinking about temperament. Writing to a friend, Mead declared, "I have to get this *Sex and Temperament* book published under the status quo and while Reo is off the scene of action or he might attack it disastrously" (Caffrey and Francis 2006: 102–103). In fact, Mead and Benedict had secretly funded a two-year grant for Fortune designed to keep him out of the country and away from Mead while, unknown to him, she was arranging their divorce (Dobrin and Bashkow 2010a) as well as writing *Sex and Temperament*. Eventually, Fortune would discover this carefully laid scheme and respond to Mead's depiction of the Arapesh. She had stated that the gentle, nonaggressive Arapesh did not have warfare. Without ever mentioning Mead by name or even citing *Sex and Temperament*, Fortune (1939) published a straightforward description of Arapesh warfare, a veiled critique that deftly undermined Mead's ethnographic credibility (Dobrin and Bashkow 2010b).

Fortune's analysis of Arapesh warfare has been supported by the work of Paul Roscoe (2003), who did fieldwork in the Arapesh area and who reviewed the published and unpublished work on the Arapesh by Mead and Fortune. Roscoe found that the Arapesh had warfare by virtually any definition of the term; he also chronicled specific historical episodes of war and noted the high number of deaths resulting from these conflicts. Arapesh men were violent and aggressive during these episodes. Roscoe surmised that because Fortune was able to venture widely in the Arapesh region, he was able to gather more and better data on warfare than Mead, whose injured ankle prevented her from traveling. He also found that, compared to warfare practiced by other groups in the area, the Arapesh may have been less warlike. And he suggested, like Dobrin and Bashkow (2010b), that Mead's broad emphasis on the gentle, nonaggressive temperament that she thought permeated Arapesh culture may have led her to minimize the presence of conflict and warfare.

Working among the Tchambuli (now Chambri) in the 1970s, Deborah Gewertz (1981,1984) also questioned Mead's characterization of male and female roles. Mead found Chambri women to be dominant and aggressive while the men were submissive and nonaggressive, engaging in art, theater, and personal adornment. Using historical, comparative, and ethnographic research, Gewertz examined the circumstances surrounding this characterization. Like Mead, Gewertz agreed that women produced the overwhelming bulk of Chambri subsistence, but she found that men controlled the political sphere of Chambri life. Like Mead, Gewertz also noted that the Chambri had been defeated in war and displaced from their village, returning only under colonial protection. While Mead observed that men were preoccupied with art and carving, presumably female endeavors, Gewertz noted that these men were engaged in restoring their traditional dwellings and artifacts that had been destroyed by war; thus, these activities were not necessarily "feminine." Gewertz also observed that Chambri women did not dominate their men or vice versa, finding that the Western categories that Mead used to characterize their relationships may have misrepresented how Chambri men and women interacted.

These restudies and critiques are relevant because *Sex and Temperament* became an influential text. Along with Benedict's *Patterns of Culture* and Mead's earlier two books on Samoa and Manus, *Sex and Temperament* was a major anthropological contribution to public discourse in the 1930s and beyond. These books also formed some of the basis of the emerging culture and personality school within anthropology during the 1930s and 1940s.

NOTES

1. On Gregory Bateson, David Lipset's (1980) biography introduces this complex figure.
2. On the "squares," Gerald Sullivan (2004) provides a solid introduction.

CHAPTER 6

CULTURE AND PERSONALITY, AND BALI

● ● ●

Although the Great Depression reduced job opportunities in anthropology and funding for research, the culture and personality school thrived in the 1930s with Mead and Benedict as key figures in its growth. Interest in the relationship between culture and the individual was strongly influenced by the psychoanalytic work of Freud, Carl Jung, and others whose ideas were popular in the 1920s, 1930s, and 1940s. Some anthropologists took more than an academic interest in psychoanalysis and were analyzed themselves, although Mead was not one of them. And psychoanalysts became deeply interested in anthropology. While figures such as Malinowski and Kroeber cautioned against the use of Freudian thinking when applied to entire cultures, others, such as Mead, Benedict, and Sapir, found psychoanalytic perspectives useful, employing neo-Freudian approaches that incorporated social and cultural differences.

Neo-Freudian theory stressed the early socialization of children in the formation of adult personality. This type of theory was more humanistic and more concerned with individual personalities than the more mechanistic psychological theories available, such as behaviorism and learning theory. Personality as a concept—with its focus on the maturing individual—was a very American concern. And the unconscious was important because, like culture, it might not be apparent to individuals or

group members but could profoundly influence thought and behavior (Sapir 1929b).

In the late 1920s and 1930s, there were overlapping circles of
involvement in the culture and personality school. At Columbia,
Mead and Benedict were at the center of one circle and were its
best-known proponents. At Yale, Sapir was at the center of another circle. Although he would suffer a heart attack in 1937 and
die in 1939, Sapir was a key figure in the development of the culture and personality school, representing anthropological interest in personality on the Social Science Research Council and the
National Research Council.

Presenting papers, publishing articles, organizing meetings,
giving seminars, and training graduate students, Sapir addressed
the same questions as Mead and Benedict. Did cultures favor certain personality types and discourage others? Could cultures be
characterized as individual personalities writ large? Why were
some cultural practices considered "normal" in some cultures
but "abnormal" in others? And what were the best ways to study
the relationship of individual personalities and cultural patterns?
Yet due to the hostile relationship between Mead and Sapir, as
well as a falling out between Benedict and Sapir, they did not collaborate but rather worked along parallel tracks. Sapir was even
reluctant to use the term "culture and personality" because of its
association with Mead and Benedict.

Still another circle in the culture and personality school, also
at Columbia, was led by psychiatrist Abram Kardiner, working
with anthropologists Cora Du Bois, Ralph Linton, and Clyde
Kluckhohn in the late 1930s and early 1940s. Whatever their differences, researchers in these different circles shared a number of
common assumptions. Individuals did not exist apart from their
culture. For cultural systems to work as integrated wholes, there
had to be close relationship between individual personalities
and their culture. How children were raised, particularly during
the lengthy period of infantile dependency, was important in
their later development. Primary socialization agents included
mothers, fathers, siblings, and other family members. Nurtured

in particular ways, including breastfeeding, toilet training, and sleeping arrangements, children grew into adulthood exhibiting a common "modal personality" or "national character." Yet the socialization processes could be imperfect, leading to deviance or possibly unresolved conflicts that might later find resolution in culturally approved institutions such as trance or initiation rites.

Of course, neo-Freudian ideas could be problematic, including the assumption that early socialization practices were critical in shaping more or less uniform adult personalities. In her study of Manus, Mead herself had found a significant discontinuity between child socialization and adult worldviews. Furthermore, the characterization of whole cultures with diagnostic labels such as "paranoid" was a questionable extension of diagnoses originally intended for individuals. For example, Benedict used Fortune's material on Dobu in *Patterns of Culture* to characterize the Dobuans as "paranoid." She did not intend this as a diagnosis of collective psychopathology since, for the Dobuans, such a configuration was culturally "normal." Nevertheless, sensing the misuse of such labels, Fortune sent Benedict a private note of concern about this characterization of the Dobuans.

Despite such problems, a large number of cultural anthropologists engaged in a great deal of culture and personality research from the 1930s through the 1960s, providing detailed ethnographic studies and sophisticated theoretical insights (Spindler 1978). Among its notable practitioners were Cora Du Bois, A. I. Hallowell, Anthony F. C. Wallace, Melford Spiro, John W. M. Whiting, and Beatrice B. Whiting. Culture and personality courses were a staple of the undergraduate and graduate curriculum in anthropology for decades. This school also produced a disproportionate number of leaders in the anthropological community. In the forty-year period between 1938 and 1978, ten members of this school would be elected president of the American Anthropological Association, including Benedict, Mead, and Sapir. Their leadership crossed disciplinary boundaries and brought together scholars in related social sciences.

INTERDISCIPLINARY WORK

By the early 1930s, Mead was probably the best-known anthropologist in the United States, and Benedict had already become one of the five leading figures in anthropology, according to the journal *Science* (Banner 2003: 292). Cultivating links to scholars in the social sciences who were also interested in the relationship between culture and personality, these two women explored this growing area of research in seminars and interdisciplinary conferences. They were now networking with psychologists, psychoanalysts, sociologists, and others, all of whom shared their interest in child socialization, adolescence, and adult personality. A number of these colleagues were or would become prominent in their own fields, including psychologists John Dollard and Gardner Murphy, psychoanalysts Eric Fromm, Karen Horney, and Erik Erikson, and sociologists Robert and Helen Lynd. Although the word "interdisciplinary" had not been coined yet, these conferences and seminars staked out new territory for the young social sciences. Culture and personality studies were becoming part of a larger interdisciplinary movement.

In the winter of 1934–35, Mead and Benedict organized one such conference around the themes of cooperation and competition. Why did some cultures seem more focused on competition while others focused on cooperation? How were children raised to become more competitive, cooperative, or individualistic? To offset the lack of funding for field research, Mead gathered a group of faculty and graduate students to look at thirteen "primitive" cultures already studied and link their character formation to other features in each culture.

She conceived the project in the following way:

To lay a background for the study of the relationship between competitive and cooperative behavior, and the problem of culture and personality, it is therefore necessary to know not only what the form of the culture is which dictates certain forms of adult behavior, but also how this adult

personality is formed in the long process of building the
cultureless infant into the adult. (1937b: 6)

The result of this conference was a volume edited by Mead titled
Cooperation and Competition among Primitive Peoples (1937b).

BALI

Throughout the 1930s and beyond, a small group of devoted
friends and colleagues helped organize, manage, and facilitate
Mead's busy career. Marie Eichelberger, one of the former Ash
Can Cats from Mead's Barnard days, was her primary organizer,
as well as the keeper of her secrets. Ruth Benedict filed Mead's
taxes, invested her book royalties, and edited her manuscripts.
Other women, some paid and some not, also provided assistance. This kind of support was essential to Mead.

In the mid-1930s, Mead's personal priority was reuniting with
Gregory Bateson. Although in England, he continued to be an
important part of her life. As well as corresponding regularly
across the Atlantic, Mead also visited Bateson in Ireland for two
weeks in 1934, and in 1935 he came to the United States from
England to give lectures and visit with Mead. In 1935, Mead's divorce from Fortune was finalized, again in Mexico, and Mead and
Bateson now were free to marry, which they did in 1936 on their
way to pursue fieldwork in Bali.

During their research among the Tchambuli, the two ethnographers had engaged in long discussions about temperaments in
the cultures they had studied. But one set of temperaments was
missing among the cultures they had mapped onto the "squares";
they thought that Bali might be that culture. So Mead and
Bateson wanted to pursue fieldwork on Balinese temperament
and character. They were also interested in schizophrenia (or bi-
polar disorder), a condition that involved psychological dissoci-
ation and was considered a form of mental illness in the West.
They saw trance in Bali as a related dissociative state. Yet, in Bali,
trance was considered normal and culturally approved at both

individual and group levels. Bateson and Mead thought the study of this culturally constituted dissociative state might cast light on schizophrenia in America.

Each ethnographer received funding for two full years, the longest period of fieldwork for either of them. In March 1936, they arrived in Bali. Mead was thirty-four, Bateson thirty-one. She thought that their matching temperaments would provide "the perfect intellectual and emotional working partnership" for fieldwork (1972: 246).

Bali was unlike any of the cultures in which they had previously worked; it was a Southeast Asian culture rather than a South Pacific culture. Bali was a highly stratified culture with literacy among the upper classes. It was a theatrical culture, filled with ritual, dance, and art. The Balinese language was widely spoken by over a million people, as opposed to a few hundred speakers for most language groups in New Guinea. The roads in the lowlands were well kept under the Dutch colonial regime, and it was relatively easy to get around, including by car. Compared to New Guinea, Mead thought that Bali was "safe" and "tame" (Caffrey and Francis 2006: 25).

Mead had lost considerable weight during each of her previous fieldwork experiences, but in Bali she did not lose any weight. The food was "delicious." She wrote her father that, "This is the most comfortable fieldwork I have ever done, no malaria, no heat, no mosquitoes, good fresh food, and no need to push anyone" (Caffrey and Francis 2006: 27).

The lowland Balinese landscape was stunningly beautiful with its terraced rice fields. Even better, there were Europeans resident in Bali who would become intellectual companions. Jane Belo, a friend of Mead's from her college days, was studying Balinese art, and her husband Colin McPhee was studying Balinese music. Walter Spies, an artist and long-time resident of Bali, was another valuable source of assistance. Unlike colonial officers and European residents in New Guinea who looked down on the "natives," these friends and colleagues admired Balinese culture and came to the island to learn from the Balinese. They helped Mead and Bateson understand Balinese culture, providing them with company, conversation, and practical assistance, including finding servants for the couple. Skilled help was readily available.

After studying the language for two months in the lowlands, Mead and Bateson chose to reside in a cool mountain village of about five hundred Balinese, where the roads were rougher and there was no terraced agriculture. They had a house built for them in Bajoeng Gedé, a poor peasant village whose people were often in compromised health and where ceremonials and rituals were less complex and elaborate than in villages elsewhere. Initially, the people of Bajoeng Gedé were suspicious of these strangers; Mead and Bateson were thought to be representatives of the Dutch colonial government or possibly wealthy tourists.

To overcome these suspicions, Mead became a local health care provider, binding wounds and tending fevers. Gradually, the villagers became more trusting and open, making this field experience an ethnographic pleasure. By simply walking through the village, Mead and Bateson could encounter a shadow play, a trance dance, or a cockfight—"sheer heaven for the anthropologist." Bateson himself owned two cocks ready for fighting. There were births and deaths, festivals and funerals. Unlike some of their New Guinea experiences, where the ethnographers had to patiently wait for ceremonials and local drama, in Bali there was a constant stream of activities. The couple also paid Balinese to perform rituals for them. In the village, they worked tirelessly, sometimes eating dinner at midnight.

Later in their fieldwork, the couple rented the palace of a former Rajah, complete with gold-handled doors, that they used as a base for the study of more elaborate, high-caste ceremonials and rituals. There were orchestral performances and Balinese opera. In the lowlands, they would also take up a third residence in a Brahman courtyard in order to study upper-caste family life, personality, and art.

To document Balinese character, Mead and Bateson pioneered what is now known as visual ethnography. Bateson would take multiple photographs and film activities while Mead wrote down the substance and context of the event that was being visually recorded. In addition, they had an invaluable Balinese male secretary who could take notes and translate in five languages, including Balinese, Malay, and English. Bateson had his own lab for developing film that could process up to sixteen hundred images in an evening.

The couple's rationale for the use of visual media drew on their recognition of the limitations of their previous work involving temperament, character, and culture. As veteran ethnographers, they admitted that such concepts were vague and "intangible." More artistic than scientific, such concepts were "far too dependent upon idiosyncratic factors or style and literary skill" of the ethnographer, as well as being difficult to duplicate and evaluate (Bateson and Mead 1942: xi). Character, temperament, and culture were abstractions. Whether using English or indigenous vocabulary, the translation of peoples' thoughts and behaviors was imprecise, open to multiple interpretations, and possible misinterpretation. The addition of photography and film was designed improve ethnographic fieldwork with better observational techniques and a new means of checking for ethnographic bias.

In this cooperative enterprise, Mead and Bateson collated photos, film, and written documentation for a more complete record of Balinese culture—a significant methodological advance. Photos were not only going to be used to illustrate their work, but became central documents in it (G. Sullivan 1999). Bateson took an astonishing twenty-five thousand photographs and shot twenty-two thousand feet of film. There could be dozens of photographs, sometimes more, of the same activity at different times and in different places. Mead and Bateson could now visually demonstrate how mothers interacted with their children in different settings or view how a birth feast appeared on different occasions.

Ultimately, they would coauthor *Balinese Character: A Photographic Analysis* (Bateson and Mead 1942), an academic book that included 759 photographs carefully laid out in multiple sections with text. Mead continued to use this visual record in *Growth and Culture: A Photographic Study of Balinese Childhood* (Mead and Macgregor 1951). And Mead and Bateson would release pioneering short ethnographic films such as *Trance and Dance in Bali* (1952) to further illustrate the usefulness of visual ethnography.

In their introduction to *Balinese Character*, Bateson and Mead stated, "This is not a book about Balinese custom, but about the Balinese—about the way in which they, as living persons, moving, standing, eating, sleeping, dancing, and going into trance, embody that abstraction (after we have abstracted it) we technically call culture" (1942: xii). They hoped that a visual record accompanied by text would offer a more grounded way of studying and depicting Balinese culture, as well as culture more generally.

At the same time and in spite of her reservations about the vagueness of concepts like character, Mead provided a lengthy analysis of Balinese character formation from infancy through childhood. Balinese mothers raised their children in considerable fear, although fatherly protections and cultural institutions like trance and dance allowed children to resolve these issues. Mead concluded:

> In these various contexts of life, the Balinese character is revealed. It is a character based on fear which, because it is learned in the mother's arms, is a value as well as a threat. It is a character curiously cut off from inter-personal relationships, existing in a state of dreamy-relaxed disassociation, with occasional intervals of non-personal concentration— in trance, in gambling, and in the practice of the arts. The Balinese carries the memory of his mother's theatrical exclamation of fear . . . but he carries also the equally strong memory of his father's protective arm. (1942a: 47–48)

Once again, Mead condensed her detailed and complex observations into broad generalizations that subsequent researchers in Bali have sometimes questioned.

IATMUL

On completion of their Balinese fieldwork in March of 1938, Mead and Bateson thought about returning to New York, while also contemplating additional research in Bali. They planned a major interdisciplinary Balinese project that would include anthropologists, sociologists, psychologists, psychiatrists, and endocrinologists, even renting the former Rajah's palace for three years as headquarters for this new project. However, the project failed to materialize. The winds of war were blowing across Europe. So Mead and Bateson decided to revisit the Iatmul in New Guinea to gather material on child-rearing that would be comparable to their Balinese material.

Like their previous New Guinea fieldwork, Iatmul fieldwork was difficult. Mead contracted malaria again; Bateson was ill much of time. There was no assistant to help with recording. There was also a drought, and this led the Iatmul to abandon most ceremonials and concentrate on crocodile hunting. Unlike Bali, Mead felt that these six months "came close to being a nightmare on the Sepik River" (1972: 260).

Working through these difficulties, the couple was able to gather enough material to contrast Iatmul and Balinese socialization practices:

The way, for instance, the Balinese mother borrowed another baby in order to send her own child into a frenzy of jealousy in contrast to the way the Iatmul mother protected her child from jealousy. . . . We could contrast the way the Balinese confined drama and action to the theater and maintained their everyday relationships placidly and evenly, never allowing children to contend even for a toy, whereas Iatmul, who struggled and screamed and quarreled in regular life, used their artistic performances to introduce moments of static beauty into their more violent lives. (Mead 1972: 261)

For Mead, the point of these observations, again, was not necessarily to theorize about them but to provide detailed data that could be used by other ethnographers and future theorists interested in child development.

Figure 6.1. Margaret Mead and Gregory Bateson typing up their fieldnotes in the "mosquito room," 1938, Iatmul, New Guinea. Courtesy of the Institute for Intercultural Studies, Inc., New York.

MOTHERHOOD

Returning to Bali for another six weeks of work, Mead was once again pregnant, and she experienced another miscarriage. Now thirty-eight and filled with regret, Mead thought she might be entering premature menopause and would never be able have a child. After the couple returned to New York, they began cataloguing their photographic and film record from Bali and Iatmul. Then, quite unexpectedly, Mead learned that she was pregnant again, and this time she was able to carry the pregnancy to term.

Mary Catherine ("Cathy") Bateson was born on 8 December 1939. It was no ordinary birth; at Mead's request there was a photographer, a film maker, and a child psychologist present to record the event, along with Dr. Benjamin Spock, a friend who would soon become the best-known pediatrician in the world. Bateson, in England at the time, was joyous at the birth of a daughter. Although the birth went smoothly, Mead experienced a recurrence of malaria and could not leave the hospital immediately.

Cathy's birth was another turning point in Mead's life. Motherhood was something she had long desired, a desire reinforced by her revulsion of Mundugumor infanticide. No longer an ethnographer who studied mothers and children, Mead was now a mother herself.

Cathy was born just months after World War II broke out in Europe, and the war required new living arrangements for the family because Mead and Bateson would be away for much of the conflict. Following Cathy's birth, the couple moved into a New York household with Bateson's two British teenage goddaughters, a nanny for Cathy, and the nanny's own daughter. During the war years, the family continued to reside communally with additional household members. The most enduring of these mixed households involved the family of Lawrence K. Frank, a member of the culture and personality school and a close friend of Mead's, who had a brownstone in Greenwich Village. Operating like an extended family, this household provided Cathy with a number of caregivers and quasi-siblings while Mead and Bateson were away due to their wartime commitments. This household would last for fifteen years.

CHAPTER 7

THE WAR YEARS AND NATIONAL CHARACTER STUDIES

● ● ●

The war took precedence over Mead's personal life and professional trajectory. The first fourteen years of her career (1925–
1939) had been consumed with fieldwork, writing popular and
professional books, and launching her public persona. During
the next period of her life (1939–1953), she would be involved
in war-related national character studies, applied projects, and
policy research.[1]

Mead had not participated in politics since the mid-1920s, not
even voting in a presidential election. During much of the Great
Depression in the 1930s, she had been out of the United States
and in the field. However, both Mead and Bateson were aware of
and disturbed by the rise of Hitler and fascism in Germany. When
World War II began in Europe in 1939, Bateson, as a British cit-
izen, left for England to see if he could assist in the war effort.
Mead was so concerned about Hitler's aggression that in August
of 1939 she wrote a letter to Eleanor Roosevelt, the president's
wife, arguing that the president should try to divert Hitler from
war by enlisting him in a pan-European peace effort. Mead opti-
mistically believed that such a peace would give Hitler "greater
glory" than war (Yans-McLaughlin 1986a: 6). However, a week
after the letter was penned, Germany invaded Poland, and World
War II in Europe began.

Although the United States was not yet involved in the war,
Mead and Bateson sensed that the country would not be able to

avoid it. In 1939, as a way of preparing for what they saw as inevitable, they joined an unofficial group called the Committee on National Morale, which consisted of intellectuals, scholars, and academic refugees from Europe who wanted to mobilize their talents in the event of war. The Committee on National Morale was particularly interested in how the social sciences could help the war effort by building American morale, not only to fight against fascism but to fight for American democracy. It was one of many such groups.

In 1939, though, most Americans were not interested in another European war; memories of World War I and the persistence of the Great Depression were major reasons for their reluctance. Polls demonstrated that Americans were overwhelmingly isolationist. Roosevelt knew war was coming, but he could not openly defy public opinion and the will of Congress. It was only after Hitler declared war on the United States in the wake of Pearl Harbor in December of 1941 that Roosevelt was able to respond by declaring war on Germany.

NATIONAL CHARACTER STUDIES

Eager to be in Washington, DC, Mead took a government position in the war effort, heading the National Research Council's Committee on Food Habits, an appointment arranged by Benedict. She was given a leave of absence from the American Museum of Natural History and from Columbia, where she had been teaching a course. While commuting between New York and Washington, Mead actively networked with anthropologists and other influential social scientists. She was also able to recruit colleagues to work for the war effort and bring young people on board who might later become anthropologists. As a national emergency, the war provided a seriousness and an immediacy to their work. In Washington, Mead hoped to expand anthropology's reach, putting the discipline on the policy map (Mandler 2013).

Economists had held sway in war policy matters, but they tended to neglect the significance of culture and the importance of cultural differences. Mead and her colleagues wanted to demonstrate how and why culture was relevant, and they raised questions that economists could not answer. They were especially interested in how allies could effectively communicate with each other despite their differences, and how current enemies might become future allies after the war.

Mead and Bateson felt that their earlier work could be useful during the war, making the case that culture and character mattered. It was in this context that national character studies emerged with Mead as its central figure (Honigmann 1967: 96). Yet the leap from village-based studies of non-Western cultures to studies of much larger, more stratified, rapidly changing, mostly Euro-American nation-states, in an international wartime context no less, was enormous. If there were problems with earlier character studies, how much more daunting would this new enterprise be? The war would provide a testing ground for culture and personality studies.

The kind of locally based fieldwork familiar to ethnographers was not an option during the war. Even before America's entry into the war, Mead, Benedict, and Bateson developed a way of looking at national character that they called the study of culture "at a distance." Anthropologists and their colleagues in other disciplines would recruit immigrants from the relevant countries studied, especially well-educated individuals who could speak knowledgeably about their own cultures. Researchers then took their life histories and gave them psychological tests, as well as examining movies, newspapers, novels, folklore, and other cultural artifacts, in order to assemble an overall portrait of a country's national character.

During the war, two new people became part of Mead's inner circle and played important roles in the development of national character studies. Geoffrey Gorer was an upper-class British intellectual who had traveled widely and written about Africa, Bali, and popular culture prior to the war. Mead had read his work, met him before going to Bali, and was immediately attracted to his keen intelligence and neo-Freudian perspective. Benedict also found Gorer a promising intellect. He was fascinated by other cultures and had independently come to think about them in terms of child rearing, sex, and adult personality.

Because Gorer was regarded as an amateur, Mead encouraged him to become more professionally oriented by doing fieldwork in the Himalayas. His ethnography, *Himalayan Village: An Account of the Lepchas of Sikkim* (1938), gave him professional credibility, although he did not earn a PhD. During the war, Gorer often resided in Washington, DC, and worked intensively with Mead and Benedict on national character studies. His memorandum on Japanese national character recommending that the Japanese emperor remain on the throne after the war so impressed officials at the U.S. Office of War Information that they offered him a position analyzing national cultures. Gorer's work on Japanese child-rearing also received public attention in an article in *Time* magazine titled "Why Are Japs Japs?" (7 August 1944).

The other person who entered Mead's life at this time was Rhoda Métraux, a young researcher who would later earn a PhD from Yale; she was also the wife of anthropologist Alfred Métraux. Métraux first worked with Mead on the Committee on Food Habits and then as an assistant to Bateson in the Office of Secret Services. She would become a key figure in national character studies and, later, Mead's life partner, housemate, and often silent coauthor from the mid-1950s until Mead's death.

As members of the culture and personality school, Mead, Benedict, Bateson, Gorer, and Métraux posited links between child socialization and adult national character, hypothesizing that child-rearing practices could have implications for adult acceptance or rejection of different political regimes. For example, if children were raised by indulgent parents with little discipline, they might become adults with an aversion to punitive authority, including totalitarian regimes, and be more welcoming of democratic rule. On the other hand, children raised under strict discipline by punitive parents might become adults who accepted authoritarian rule and whose frustrated childhoods might lead them to greater aggression in adulthood as well as greater acceptance of authoritarian propaganda. This way of looking at national character was thought to be nonideological and hence nonpolitical, a potential virtue in the highly politicized wartime environment. Such ideas were then applied to qualitative national character studies of Germany, Japan, and the Soviet Union, as well as Greece, the Netherlands, and Burma.

AMERICAN CHARACTER

Mead herself focused on American national character, authoring a popular book, *And Keep Your Powder Dry* (1942b), to harness American morale for the war effort. The book was written in three weeks in the summer of 1942. In it, she acknowledged that thinking about "national character" had fallen into disrepute since the end of World War I, but that World War II had revived interest. Mead later stated that the book was "a social scientist's contribution to winning the war and establishing a just and lasting peace." She explained, "It was frankly and completely partisan . . . to present the culture and character of my own people in a way they would find useful and meaningful in meeting the harsh realities of war" (1965 preface: xxxi).

In her book, Mead asked, "What then is this American character, this expression of American institutions and of American attitudes which is embodied in every American, in everyone born in this country and sometimes even in those who have come later to these shores?" (1942b: 17). She emphasized how understanding ourselves, not just the Germans and Japanese, was essential to winning the war, writing, "This war must be made to make sense to us, as a people, if we are to fight and win it; and then work to keep all that we have gained. We must fight it like Americans from the start . . . sure of our direction, and therefore sure of our ultimate victory" (1942b: 105). Mead thought that it was necessary to fight and win the war in the "right" way—that is, by marshaling the strengths of American character, as well as American democratic institutions. She rejected the use of authoritarian measures in defense of democracy. To this end, she catalogued the strengths that she saw in American character, such as the belief in equality regardless of race, sex, or class, and a belief in finding common ground amid differences.

Mead saw Nazi Germany not only in terms of its dictatorial leader, but also in terms of a people whose character was different from the character of Americans. The positive American values that separated Americans and Germans included using aggression as a response to external forces rather than as an end in itself, employing violence for altruistic rather than selfish purposes, and viewing war as a temporary condition leading to peace rather than a permanent strategy for national expansion.

Mead looked for commonalities as well as differences in national character, arguing that the odds for a permanent peace after the war were better achieved by understanding both. She did not want to demonize, vilify, or stereotype the German people; Mead and her colleagues wanted to know how the character of German men and women, husbands and wives, parents and children, families and institutions, as well as Hitler and the Nazi party, might affect the outcome of the war and its aftermath.

And Keep Your Powder Dry was well received. Mead's timing was prescient since America had just entered the war. However, she would later acknowledge that some of the book sounded like a call to arms. And the book's analysis of American character, insightful as it may have been, was impressionistic, intuitive, and anecdotal. These were the very problems with earlier character studies that Mead and Bateson acknowledged in *Balinese Character*.

Mead's sweeping generalities about American national character avoided discussion of the Deep South, with its history of slavery, Jim Crow, and discrimination. In a footnote, she noted that her analysis was based only on Americans in the North, Middle West, and West (1942b: 14). Mead understood that there were differences among Americans, referring to American character in terms of "ordered heterogeneity," but stressing uniformity over difference.

Academic considerations aside, Mead realized the life-and-death stakes in the war, the importance of morale building, and the necessity of national unity. The war brought together conservatives and liberals who were otherwise opposed. Moreover, Mead and her colleagues recognized there were, indeed, substantial differences between Germany, Japan, and the United States that needed to be understood whatever the shortcomings of national character studies. Thus, she threw herself into the war effort, working in government agencies, doing war-related research, giving public talks, and appearing on radio and in magazines to motivate everyday citizens.

APPLYING ANTHROPOLOGY

The problems that would involve wartime research led Mead and her colleagues to found the Society for Applied Anthropology in 1941 even before the United States entered the war. With so many anthropologists becoming concerned with practical applications of anthropological knowledge, it seemed that a less academic and more applied organization than the American Anthropological Association was needed.

During the war years, about half of American anthropologists worked in U.S. government programs on problems that required a certain kind of "social engineering," as Mead put it. Government officials thought anthropological expertise could be of value in the war effort, especially language skills and cultural knowledge based on ethnographic research in various areas of the world. War against the Japanese in the Pacific meant that Mead and others who knew about Pacific cultures could teach short courses to military personnel about to be deployed to that region.

At the National Research Council's Committee on Food Habits, Mead was concerned with key aspects of American food production and distribution. Food had to be rationed during the war, but how should scarce food resources be allocated? Should everyone be provided with the same foods? Mead and her colleagues argued that different ethnic groups and different regions in the U.S. had different preferences, and these had to be taken into account. To provide food that people wanted to eat, teams of researchers discussed shoppers' preferences with them. Rather than imposing diets on people, Mead saw this a more democratic way of solving the problem. Providing food abroad during and after the war required the same consumer-based orientation.

Market forces also had to be factored into food allocation, and these had to be effectively communicated to consumers. Housewives were encouraged to buy more dairy products than usual in 1942 because, if dairying was unprofitable, herds might be sold off and less meat and milk would be available in the future. Mead and her colleagues learned to translate macroeconomic food policy issues into language that housewives could understand. During the war, neighborhood block leaders were responsible for getting these messages across.

On a different applied issue, Mead was sent to England to solve a problem involving American soldiers who were going out with English women. With large numbers of American servicemen in England—over one and a half million in 1944—there was an increase in the number of unwanted pregnancies, as well as accusations of "immorality" on both sides. Since Great Britain was a key ally in the war, this problem had to be addressed. In England, Mead found a mismatch between the sexual expectations of American men and English women. American men expected English women to set limits on sexual activity just as American women did in the United States. However, English women expected American men to set their own limits on sexual activity just as English men did in England. These differing expectations about who was responsible for saying "yes" and "no" were the problem. Mead authored a wartime pamphlet, gave radio talks and lectures, and provided role-playing assignments to resolve this situation.

In England, Mead was extremely popular as a lecturer. On tour, she drew audiences of up to a thousand people at a time. With her flair for public speaking, Mead's radio broadcasts were also popular. *And Keep Your Powder Dry* was republished in England as *The American Character*. Until the war, Mead had spent little time in the country and knew relatively few British citizens apart from Bateson and Gorer. As she interacted with ordinary British citizens, she quickly grew to love them, and their character became more apparent to her. Recognizing the differences between Americans and the English underscored Mead's focus on the importance of cross-cultural communication. She reiterated that national character studies were vital for communicating with close allies as well as combatting deadly enemies.

TOP SECRET WORK

During the war, a number of anthropologists, including Mead, Bateson, and Métraux, also worked in top-secret and psychological warfare capacities in the Office of Secret Services (OSS), a forerunner of the CIA. Bateson was sent to Southeast Asia for twenty months, working in counterintelligence against the Japanese, and broadcasting "black propaganda" intended to undermine the Japanese. He also volunteered for a perilous mission to rescue three OSS agents who escaped from their captors deep in Japanese territory during the summer of 1945 (Price 2008: 239–243). Bateson was awarded the Asiatic-Pacific Campaign Service Ribbon for his bravery and willingness to partake in this mission. Nevertheless, his participation in the war took a toll. Bateson also had misgivings about producing wartime propaganda, and so did Mead (Price 2016: 74). In their eyes, it was dishonest and could hurt the postwar agenda of building a lasting peace.

Mead's participation and leadership in wartime work and national character projects enhanced her academic profile. At Harvard, anthropologist Clyde Kluckhohn and sociologist Talcott Parsons, both of whom had worked with Mead, held her in such high regard that they tried to recruit her as a faculty member, along with Bateson. However, at the time, the president of Harvard did not want to hire a woman professor (Gilkeson 2009: 262). Mead remained a part-time faculty member at Columbia.

THE MORALITY OF WARTIME ANTHROPOLOGY

In the post–Vietnam War era, ethical questions have been posed about the participation of anthropologists in wartime projects. However, the war was a crisis in which almost no one could claim neutrality; it had to be won. Cultural relativism was all well and good as a perspective for studying other cultures. So was the appreciation of cultural differences with each culture having its own set of values and practices that needed to be understood on their own terms. Although cultural relativism was a research tool requiring temporary suspension of moral and ethical judgments, if all such judgments were considered to be of equal value, the result would be moral and political paralysis. Japan and Germany had declared war on the United States. Mead and Bateson understood the threat of fascism and chose to work for the American government, as did most other anthropologists and social scientists.

These were not easy choices, and they came with an emotional price. The pressures of war, their different missions, and long separations eroded the Mead-Bateson relationship. With Mead in England and Washington, DC, much of the time, and Bateson in Southeast Asia, the couple saw little of each other and not enough of their daughter. Putting the pieces of their lives back together would be difficult. Bateson was depressed, exhausted, and disillusioned. After a year together in New York City, the couple gradually separated. Bateson eventually left New York for Harvard and then California. They would amicably divorce in Mexico in 1950. Unlike her previous two divorces, Mead did not initiate the proceedings, and she was despondent over the end of their marriage. Nonetheless, they continued to have a good working relationship.

NATIONAL CHARACTER STUDIES AFTER THE WAR

During the war, the government restricted circulation of most national character studies, but after the war a number were published. The most prominent of these was Ruth Benedict's *The Chrysanthemum and the Sword* (1946), a study of Japanese character at a distance done for the Office of War Information. Benedict did not study the Japanese language, nor had she been to Japan; for some of her research, she interviewed Japanese Americans and Japanese in the United States, but most of her knowledge was secondhand. Immediately after the war, Benedict attempted to go to Japan to study the culture firsthand, but was barred from doing so by the American military that occupied postwar Japan over fears of allegedly predatory Japanese men. Male researchers had no such restrictions.

In her study of Japanese national character, Benedict captured the peaceful (the chrysanthemum) and aggressive (the sword) sides of Japanese culture, encouraging readers to appreciate Japanese cultural differences and respect a defeated enemy. She also supported a noninterventionist approach by the American occupiers in postwar Japan, regarding wholesale changes to Japanese culture as counterproductive to peacetime reconstruction. Like Mead, Benedict was interested in a world that accepted cultural differences.

Although not immediately popular in the United States, *The Chrysanthemum and the Sword* eventually sold hundreds of thousands of copies here, with more than two million additional copies sold in postwar Japan itself. In the 1950s, many Japanese were familiar with Benedict's book. In America, the book's success led to the reissue of *Patterns of Culture*, her other million-seller, further popularizing the idea that each culture had its own configuration that needed to be appreciated on its own terms.

The Chrysanthemum and the Sword did not mention the first use of atomic bombs on Hiroshima and Nagasaki that ended World War II in the Pacific. Yet "the bomb" changed everything for Benedict and Mead; the possibility of nuclear annihilation on a global scale meant that the pursuit of peace was more urgent than ever. For these women and a number of their wartime colleagues, their research on national character would move seamlessly into the immediate postwar era. As a result of the war, the culture and personality approach and national character studies became part of a major interdisciplinary movement with anthropology as its center of gravity. The discipline was now taken seriously in policy circles.

THE RESEARCH ON
CONTEMPORARY CULTURES PROJECT

After the war, Benedict channeled her expertise on national character and commitment to world peace into a major research project at Columbia University. The U.S. Office of Naval Research provided $100,000 to fund the program on Research on Contemporary Cultures, whose participants included Mead, Bateson, Gorer, and Métraux. Mead assisted Benedict in administering this huge, multiyear enterprise with a staff of 120 from fourteen different disciplines. In terms of personnel, this was the largest peacetime project ever run by anthropologists. The RAND Corporation contributed additional funding for a study of the Soviet Union, bringing the project's overall funding to a quarter of a million dollars.

When the Columbia project commenced in 1947, the Cold War between the Soviet Union and the West had already begun. The Iron Curtain had descended on Eastern Europe, and the struggle between communism and democracy made fieldwork in that part of the world impossible. Even for those noncommunist cultures where fieldwork could still be done, project leaders preferred studying each culture "at a distance" because they did not want the project or its participants to be perceived as spying by the U.S. government or involving national security issues. This research was therefore unclassified.

Despite the potential military confrontation between the USSR and the West, Mead and Benedict believed their studies would assist in the peaceful quest for "one world, many cultures." They hoped that national differences would be mutually understood and that common interests would prevail, a line of thinking that was mirrored in international organizations such as the United Nations. Yet Benedict did not live to see the results of the Contemporary Cultures Project. She died in 1948 at age sixty-one, another devastating loss for Mead.

After Benedict's death, Mead became the leader of the project, focusing on studies of Russia, France, Czechoslovakia, Poland, and Syria, and of Eastern European Jews. No longer a lone ethnographer in Samoa or member of a small, village-based research team in New Guinea and Bali, Mead was now administering a very large and influential research center. Once an individual participant-observer and fieldworker, she was now employing the study of culture at a distance on a grand interdisciplinary scale with multiple colleagues, including anthropologists Eric Wolf, Francis L. K. Hsu, Conrad Arensberg, and Ruth Bunzel. Clyde Kluckhohn, who worked with Mead during the war, was directing a similar project at Harvard's Russian Research Center. Anthropologists were now significant figures in international affairs.

Although there had been team research in earlier national character studies, the postwar Contemporary Cultures Project often used large teams of ten or more people and used them much more systematically. Mead emphasized this aspect of the project:

> We have learned to work in groups, so that workers of both sexes, different types of background, and training may bring their combined insight to bear on the material which is gathered and prepared for each [culture]. We have tried to make it a rule to include in each working group, members of the culture which we are studying as well as members of other cultures, to ensure the type of understanding which comes from combining deep personal participation in a culture with the insights that come from contrast, and from disciplined anthropological methods. (1952: 15)

Another innovation was the nonhierarchical organization of the project to allow for more creative thinking.

As the Contemporary Cultures Project developed, its sheer size made it somewhat unwieldy, and the methodological issues of studying culture at a distance continued to be thorny. The assumption that early childhood socialization shaped adult personality and therefore national character remained intriguing, but was still far from demonstrated. The concept of national character itself suggested a singular and more or less uniform set of child rearing practices and adult personalities. But how could such uniformity be measured? Mead preferred a qualitative approach employing a small number of individuals that the research team knew well rather than using statistical sampling or polling a broad range of people. Yet such a qualitative approach to studies of large, highly stratified nations could be even more problematic than in the study of smaller non-Western cultures. Mead addressed this problem by stating that "any member of a group, provided his position within the group is properly specified, is a perfect sample of the groupwide pattern on which he is acting as an informant" (1953: 658). This position seemed to assume that the groupwide pattern was already known.

Meanwhile, research on Native Americans was questioning the very idea of national character itself. Anthony F. C. Wallace's study of Tuscarora and Ojibwa national character, the most sophisticated study of its kind for that period, found that less than 40 percent of the Tuscarora population fit a "modal" personality. Wallace concluded that "the problems of personality and culture are almost terrifying in their complexity. The national characters of two small societies have been analyzed and compared; the task required almost as much conceptual formulation as manipulation of actual data . . . only a beginning has been made" (1952: 110). His study once again raised the question, just how close was the relationship between individuals and their culture? Was there a homogenous "replication of uniformity" among individuals or was there, rather, a more differentiated "organization of diversity"? (Wallace 1961).

THE SWADDLING HYPOTHESIS

Critics of national character studies felt that there was too much interest in child socialization and culture, and not enough interest in power, ideology, and history (Mandler 2013). Geoffrey

Gorer's study of Russian national character illustrated this point and would reflect negatively on the entire national character enterprise. Mead had recruited Gorer to colead the study of Russian national character of which she was part. With a proven track record based on his wartime research, Mead liked Gorer's thinking about child socialization. After Bateson's departure, she even viewed Gorer as a marriage possibility, at least momentarily.

Gorer explored the Russian material with the help of a dozen research collaborators and became interested in the idea that Russian national character—or, more accurately, only Great Russian national character—might be linked to the practice of infant swaddling. Great Russian babies were tightly bound in blankets to swaddling boards and cribs, except during nursing. Gorer hypothesized that this practice prevented free movement and independence, and was possibly linked to cold, dependent, and authoritarian adult personalities.

Along with restrictive swaddling during the first several months of infancy, Gorer noted that Great Russian babies were generously breastfed, although without strong emotional attachment to their mothers. Toilet training came later and was neither strict nor punitive. According to Gorer, this combination of denial of affection on the one hand and indulgence on the other could be associated with an adult syndrome of fear and guilt, depression and rage, with gratification sought in excessive drinking, feasting, and sex. This association of child-rearing practices and adult personality came to be known as the "swaddling hypothesis," a hypothesis that Mead supported. She herself had studied a similar practice in Bali, and Benedict provided a comparative study of swaddling throughout eastern Europe.

Gorer was careful to state his biases, how the research was done, and its tentative nature and limitations. He cautioned that swaddling was simply one of a number of ways that Great Russian parents communicated with their children; that is, swaddling did not cause adult personality—positions also held by Mead (G. Sullivan 2009). Yet phrasing the hypothesis in this more nuanced manner did not strengthen the argument nor did it appease its critics.

After reading Gorer's initial report in an obscure journal, Russian experts and other critics immediately challenged the hypothesis. Gorer had not been able to study how widespread swaddling actually was among Great Russians or how homogenous adult Great Russian personalities really were; there may have been considerable variability in both. In addition, there were no longitudinal studies of Great Russian child-rearing and resulting adult personalities. Moreover, such studies would have had to recognize the political and ideological repercussions of the Russian revolution and the Stalinist period that attempted to produce a "New Socialist Man."

Gorer's conclusions had policy implications. His hypothesis suggested that the authoritarian culture resulting, in part, from swaddling would be difficult to change and that the Russian intelligentsia and elites saw "potential enemies all around them" (Gorer and Rickman 1949: 190). According to Gorer, it was essential to understand that Russians were suspicious of the West and would seek to exploit Western weaknesses. While some of these conclusions were undoubtedly true, they were obvious and hardly new. Moreover, his conclusions about the authoritarian culture of the Great Russian masses were not necessarily what American policy makers were interested in hearing (Mandler 2013). They wanted to hear that Russians craved freedom, just like people in the West, cultural differences be damned. The commercial publication of *The People of Great Russia* (1949) by Gorer and John Rickman did little to dampen criticism. In the meantime, Mead, surprised by the criticism, continued to defend the swaddling hypothesis. She considered Gorer among the most valuable participants in national character studies.

Criticism of the hypothesis appeared not only in the American press; both Gorer and Mead were taken to task in the Soviet newspaper *Isvestia*. For critics, the swaddling hypothesis embodied an unfortunate application of psychoanalytic ideas that was now openly mocked as "diaperology." Critics wondered, was the hypothesis a key to understanding Russian national character or a merely caricature of it?

Gorer was acutely aware of the problems inherent in national character studies, especially in the context of the Cold War. He hoped his modest contribution would help avoid a nuclear war with the Soviet Union. As he explained in 1950,

> Were the political situation not so desperate, it would probably be more desirable to wait another 50 years, while the techniques of anthropology, sociology, and psychology were further refined and elaborated before attempting so complex and difficult a task with such relatively inadequate tools. But we do not have a choice; we are not even certain that we have another 50 years. (Gorer 1961: 258)

In the political environment of the Cold War, Gorer's approach to national character was an embarrassment. For Cold War ideologues, the problem wasn't character; it was communism. Mead's superiors on the project told her in no uncertain terms to minimize or eliminate the swaddling hypothesis in her own work on Russian character. As a result, her book *Soviet Attitudes towards Authority* (1951a) contained very little on child socialization. It was also similar to other works on the Soviet Union from that period rather than being distinctly anthropological.

The swaddling hypothesis should have been a minor chapter in national character studies, but it was symptomatic of larger problems in this body of work and, by implication, culture and personality studies. Because Mead had defended Gorer and the hypothesis (Mead 1954), and because she was so closely associated with national character studies more generally, her credibility and the credibility of culture and personality studies suffered a dramatic decline in academic and policy circles. As anthropologist Robert LeVine reported, "There followed a sweeping rejection of culture and personality theory and research in the social sciences, even by some who had previously contributed to it, so that since the 1950s the field of study has come to be stigmatized as consisting of vulgar journalistic simplifications of complex realities of social structure and culture" (1973: viii). Mead herself would abandon national character studies in the mid-1950s.

While this chapter in Mead's career is relatively unknown, especially compared to her earlier work, she devoted over a decade of her life to national character studies in a central leadership role and saw them as a logical extension of her earlier work on non-Western cultures. For a time, these studies were significant in policy circles. Yet even with substantial support from the government and intensive work with her interdisciplinary colleagues, such studies were becoming an intellectual dead end. Alex Inkeles, the noted sociologist who worked with Mead on the Contemporary Cultures Project and who also worked on the Russian project at Harvard, concluded his appraisal of national character studies in the following way: "With very few exceptions, the available studies of modal or group personality unfortunately suffer from several defects which make them poor evidence in support of *any* systematic proposition. . . . Most of these studies, therefore, are obviously of limited usefulness to the student of politics" (1961: 199).

As models for future research, national character studies were also out of favor among a younger generation of anthropologists emerging in the immediate post–World War II era. (Mandler 2013). This new generation was not interested in national character studies because they did not involve "real" fieldwork; the study of culture at a distance was regarded as an armchair enterprise in contrast to genuine participant-observation. Younger fieldworkers were more interested in non-Western cultures, not the relatively familiar Western cultures that sociologists and political scientists studied. They also wanted more rigor and precision than national character studies had employed. And, politically, they were wary of direct involvement with the national security state. "Pure" research was more desirable.

NOTE

1. On this period in Mead's life, I have drawn heavily on Peter Mandler's *Return from the Natives: How Margaret Mead Won the Second World War and Lost the Cold War* (2013) as well as Mandler (2009), Price (2008, 2016), and Yans-McLaughlin (1986a and 1986b).

CHAPTER 8

THE POSTWAR YEARS AND MANUS REVISITED

● ● ●

Even during the war, Mead continued her engagement with a broad American public and as a role model for young women. With her combination of intelligence and fame, she was a stellar example of an independent woman with her own career and opinions. In 1943, Mead was listed as one of the eight "outstanding women in the modern world" (Lutkehaus 2008: 211). In the postwar years, she amplified her public presence in articles that appeared in a variety of women's magazines, including *House Beautiful, Mademoiselle, Seventeen, Family Circle*, and *Parents Magazine*. Although Mead did not consider herself a feminist at this point in her life, many young women thought she was.

MALE AND FEMALE

After the war, Mead authored another bestselling book on sex roles. *Male and Female: A Study of the Sexes in a Changing World* (1949) returned to the topic she had first explored in *Sex and Temperament in Three Primitive Societies*. In that book, Mead demonstrated that definitions of masculinity and femininity varied across cultures and were more rooted in cultural differences than in universal biological processes. In *Male and Female*, she revisited these differences, summarizing her findings from the cultures she had studied and updating her position on the roles of biology and culture.

In a chapter titled "Basic Regularities in Human Sexual Development," biological universals were now given a more prominent role, and these included conception, puberty, pregnancy, birth, the mother-infant bond, "the child's sense of its own sex membership," and death (1949: 113–126). Mead noted:

> Different as are the ways in which different cultures pattern the development of human beings, there are basic regularities that no known culture has yet been able to evade. After excursions into contrasting educational methods of seven different societies, we can sum up the regularities that must be reckoned with by every society. Every attempt to understand what is happening in our own society, or in other societies, every attempt to understand ourselves, or to build a different life for our children, must take these into account. (1949: 113)

In *Male and Female*, Mead explored the "maternal instinct," how childbearing confirmed "femininity," and inherent differences between men and women. Had she changed her views about the relative importance of biology and culture? Some reviewers hailed this apparent change as a sensible return to conventional wisdom about "basic" sex roles. Others wondered what had happened to the Margaret Mead who wrote *Sex and Temperament*. Yet Mead's views on the interaction of biology and culture developed over her long career. In her early work, Mead argued that human nature was extremely malleable, but her views on human nature evolved over four decades during which the political and intellectual climate changed dramatically. Thus, when arguing against racial and exclusively "biological" explanations that were common in the early twentieth century and that were at the core of Nazi ideology, Mead emphasized culture. When discussing sex roles in the middle of the twentieth century, biology received more attention. Mead remarked that these two approaches to man—one of which sees man as a creature with species-characteristic instinctual patterns that play a continuing part in the forms that civilizations take, and the other which views man as lacking species-characteristic behavior patterns and as capable of being conditioned to almost any kind of system that takes into account survival needs—cross and recross each other. The optimism of the Watsonian [conditioning] position in the 1920s has been tempered by the experience of the following three decades, during which [totalitarian] "techniques" of conditioning were used in the service of absolute or irresponsible power. (1964: 10–11)

Thus, for Mead there was no contradiction between *Sex and Temperament* on the one hand and *Male and Female* on the other. She maintained that both books presented a range of human potentials. In the same year that *Male and Female* was published, the Associated Press named Mead its "Outstanding Woman of Science."

MANUS REVISITED

In the mid-1950s, Mead saw her life moving in a number of different directions. She was divorced from Bateson and missing the intellectual companionship of Benedict. At this time, Mead and Rhoda Métraux established a household of their own. And she began to think about more fieldwork. After visiting Australia to explore research possibilities, Mead decided to return to Pere, the site of her fieldwork with Fortune in 1928–29. The Admiralty Islands, of which Manus and Pere were a part, had been the site of a major military battle between American and Japanese forces during World War II; it was a crucial battleground for control of air and sea bases in that part of the South Pacific. The Japanese had occupied Manus, including a military outpost in Pere, which was later bombed. It took the Americans eighty days to defeat the Japanese in this island campaign. Manus then became a major

American staging area for the continuing war against the Japanese. Hundreds of thousands of American troops moved through the island to other arenas of conflict in the Pacific.

Mead wondered what had happened to the people of Pere and their culture as the result of the war. With all of the devastation and upheaval, had they been able to recover? Or had the war destroyed the culture and left it in shambles? Mead also wondered what had happened to the children of Pere whom she had studied twenty-five years earlier. She had not been in contact with them, nor they with her. To find out, Mead proposed a study of change in Pere, with a special emphasis on the young adults she had known as children, viewing the village as a microcosm of the postwar world.

For this research, Mead hoped to collaborate with graduate students, advertising this fieldwork opportunity among prestigious graduate programs. She was looking for students interested in the culture and personality approach who also had skills in photography and film, which had proven so valuable in her Balinese work. Ted Schwartz, a graduate student at the University of Pennsylvania, was the only person who applied. Along with his fiancé Lenora Shargo, who was an artist, Schwartz spent an intensive six months with Mead preparing for fieldwork in Manus.

For Mead, more productive fieldwork now required not only mastering conventional techniques of observation and taking fieldnotes, but also recording with photography, film, and sound, administering psychological tests, and cross-referencing all of this material to provide a more complete documentary record. Each observation/interview/event would be tracked so that the total context could be understood in terms of date, time, people present, substance, and other activities occurring simultaneously. The field team could then check the extent to which the ethnographers' observations and notes corresponded with the photo and film record.

Traveling by plane, Mead and the now-married Schwartzes arrived in Manus in July 1953. As they settled in, a nearby volcano erupted, temporarily putting fieldwork on hold. Nevertheless, Mead and her coworkers would soon become aware of the magnitude of the changes wrought during the war and thereafter. Pere was no longer a village on stilts in the lagoon; most people now lived in neat Western-style houses row by row on the shore. There was a council of elected officials. The schoolteacher, who had been a baby in 1928, asked Mead to help her teach the children of Pere. Some villagers were now literate. And everyone seemed interested in becoming part of the modern world. The devastation Mead had anticipated was nowhere in sight.

Fieldwork itself went well. Mead had a house in the center of Pere, while the Schwartzes resided with another group on Manus. They met frequently to share their experiences, becoming "like family." Mead ran a clinic every morning and was available for medical emergencies. The Schwartzes also became healthcare providers. Although Mead experienced bouts of malaria, due to medical advances they were far less debilitating than those during her earlier fieldwork in Pere. Renewing old relationships and building new ones energized Mead. She would spend six months on Manus before returning to New York; the Schwartzes continued their work for an additional six months. Together they chronicled the changes that had occurred both during and after the war.

WORLD WAR II ON MANUS

During the war, the American occupation produced "a tremendous spectacle, as miles and miles were packed with barracks . . . . The Americans knocked down mountains, blasted channels, smoothed the islands for airstrips, tore up miles of bush—all with their marvelous 'engines'" (Mead 1956: 168). Huge planes and ships disgorged trucks, bulldozers, guns, and other forms of military equipment and material wealth. For the people of Manus, there were only questions. Who were these men? Where had all of this "cargo" come from? And to whom did it belong?

In keeping with their religious beliefs about the role of ghosts and ancestral spirits, the people of Manus reasoned that the cargo belonged to their ancestors and that they were the rightful heirs to this wealth. The ghosts of their ancestors would deliver the cargo to them in a new millennium. An apocalyptic movement swept across the island, envisioning a future of abundance, but only if the old ways were abandoned. In the excitement surrounding this "cargo cult," people destroyed their own property, including shell money, mourning costumes, pottery, baskets, bedding, and clothing, in anticipation of a new order. Accompanied by ecstatic visions, they rejected traditional marriage customs, ceremonies, and membership in the Catholic Church (which had missionized the area decades earlier). They then waited for the ghosts of their ancestors to bring them the cargo that they were prepared to receive.

The cargo did not materialize, but about the same time a new, more secular, movement appeared in the area, spearheaded by a charismatic indigenous leader named Paliau. The Paliau movement was thoroughly "modern." It turned out that the Americans had more to offer than cargo; they also brought the people of Manus a new way of seeing themselves. Unlike administrative officers from previous colonial regimes in the region, the American military seemed to treat the people of Manus as equals and like "brothers" (Mead 1956: 168). The Americans did not call them "niggers" but rather "Joes" or "good Joes" (Mead 1956: 170). The people of Manus saw white people and black people—people like themselves—wearing the same uniform. And wartime hospitals demonstrated to the people of Manus the value of both black and white lives (Mead 1956: 173). The people of Manus did not view the Americans as exploiters or themselves as exploited; the appearance of equality and brotherhood led the followers of Paliau to rethink their future.

The traditional life of older adults no longer held appeal for the young people of Manus; the world of ghosts, spirits, and arranged marriages was no longer viable. So, under the leadership of Paliau, people moved from the lagoon to the shore, promoted cooperation between previously hostile groups, and encouraged people to think of themselves as part of the modern world, seeking economic opportunity and political representation. They created their own treasury for savings, established their own governing councils, reinvented their own version of Christianity, built their own schools, and changed their child-rearing practices. This almost totally new way of living was not imposed on them; they were not "victims of progress." Together they had chosen to embrace rapid and all-encompassing change—change that Mead found "astonishing and amazing" because it was occurring within a single generation.

In this new environment, Mead was no longer a foreign researcher; she was now a valuable resource and consultant—someone that people of Pere could use as a bridge to the wider world of which they were now members. She became particularly close to John Kilipak, whom she had known initially from her stay in 1928–29. Their friendship developed into genuine collaboration in which they exchanged ideas and information. In addition to being a participant-observer, Mead became a change agent in this unusual social experiment, describing her new role and detailing the story of change on Manus in her popular book, *New Lives for Old* (1956).

Mead continued to revisit Manus several times in the 1960s and 1970s with Schwartz and additional collaborators, witnessing the ongoing changes in Pere and encouraging the people along lines that she thought most productive. For example, Mead promoted the teaching of English in preparation for Manus's political participation in the new nation of Papua New Guinea, which gained its independence in 1975. An important documentary film, *Margaret Mead's New Guinea Journal* (1968), shown on public television, recorded her long and deep involvement in the lives of Pere villagers.

Although Mead would also briefly return to some of her other field sites, her enduring relationship with the people of Pere was unique in her long career and in how the people of Manus saw her. Schwartz, her long-term collaborator, stated,

> To a remarkable degree, she earned the friendship, loyalty, and almost total cooperation of the Manus people: and more, I think they loved her in a way unprecedented in

their experience. At the same time, they sometimes cringed under her disapproval; for Mead did not condescend: she was very much herself with the Manus, approving or scolding them, as she did with her colleagues at professional meetings, offering advice and intervening on their behalf with the Australian administration . . . . When news of her death arrived the village went into prolonged mourning in a manner appropriate to the death of a great chief. (Tuzin and Schwartz 1980: 246)

AFTERMATH

For a time, the rapid and positive postwar transformation of Pere made this culture a focus of attention in the West and even the United Nations. Pere was a "good news" story. As the story continued, though, it became clear that that traditions had not been entirely abandoned, that there was dissension over Paliau's role, and that Paliau's own views were changing (M. C. Bateson 1984: 174–196).

In the 1980s and 1990s, the value of Mead's research in Pere was questioned by prominent citizens from the newly independent nation of Papua New Guinea, although not from Pere itself. Nahau Rooney, a former Minister of Justice in the Papua New Guinea government, believed that Mead took from Manus more than she gave, and that some of her characterization of Manus was inaccurate (Gilliam 1992). Rooney also felt that Mead's emphasis on the "Western" aspects of the Paliau movement neglected its anti-colonial origins.

Warilea Iamo, an anthropologist from Papua New Guinea who received his PhD from the University of California, Berkeley, echoed Rooney's view that Mead patronized New Guinea people, idealizing them as "people without history" and believing that Western conceptions of economic and political development were necessary for progress without considering the sometimes turbulent colonial history of Papua New Guinea (Iamo 1992).

These criticisms of Mead and, more broadly, of anthropology, were given full voice in another PBS documentary, *Anthropology on Trial* (1983).

Questions about the value of Mead's work and Western anthropology were overshadowed more recently by a human rights drama involving the government of Papua New Guinea, the government of Australia, and Manus. The island became notorious as a detention center for refugees from Asia and elsewhere seeking asylum in Australia. In 2001, Australia negotiated an agreement with the government of Papua New Guinea to house hundreds of asylum seekers, including children, in secret, prison-like conditions on Manus for indefinite periods of time, a policy designed to deter additional asylum seekers to Australia.

The conditions on Manus were so appalling that they led to international condemnation of Australia. Early in their incarceration, prisoners rioted; local police and civilians responded with force. Dozens of detainees were injured, some severely, and one detainee was killed. There was also physical and sexual abuse of the prisoners. Despairing over the conditions of their years-long detention, more than two dozen asylum seekers attempted suicide by cutting their wrists, hanging themselves, or setting themselves on fire.

At its peak, the Manus facility housed 1,353 prisoners in an unhealthy and dangerous environment, leading to condemnation by the United Nations. The Supreme Court of Papua New Guinea finally terminated the agreement with Australia, and the program ended in 2019 with many of the refugees able to gain admission to countries other than Australia (Boochani 2019).

Thus, over several decades, the narrative about Manus changed from a story about the education of "primitive" children to a chronicle about World War II and the island's postwar development to, most recently, a postcolonial human rights nightmare.

CHAPTER 9

MEAD AS A PUBLIC FIGURE

● ● ●

From the mid-1950s until her death in 1978, Mead was busy in so many different public and professional capacities that it is difficult to provide a coherent account for this period in her life. Mead herself offered none. Unlike the first decades of her career, which followed a familiar pattern with discrete episodes of ethnographic fieldwork and publication, and unlike the years of war-related work and national character studies, Mead's last decades had many more moving parts and were lived primarily in the public sphere. These decades were less anthropological and are less easy to portray.

Mead was now spending most of her time at home in New York, although she did travel the globe revisiting some of her earlier field sites and visiting still other cultures for brief periods of time. As a senior spokesperson for anthropology, Mead was more than that; she was an icon and oracle, a public intellectual offering her knowledge and opinions on any number of issues in any number of forums, including prominent magazines such as *Fortune*, *New York Times Magazine*, the *Nation*, and the *New Republic*. Mead herself was the subject of many articles and news stories, including a profile in the *New Yorker*. In 1970, she was recognized by *Time* magazine as one of the one hundred most influential people in the world.

Mead actively cultivated her public presence for a variety of audiences through activities that included writing books and articles, teaching classes, fulfilling museum responsibilities, appearing on radio and television, accepting visiting appointments and guest lectureships, providing leadership roles, receiving various honors, and delivering keynote addresses at meetings, professional seminars, and conferences. In a typical year, Mead might give over one hundred talks to many different kinds of audiences, traveling extensively at home and abroad despite ongoing health concerns. Her weight had increased to over 170 pounds on her slight frame. And her ankle—broken and reinjured a number of times—required support. Mead did not want to use a cane; instead, she acquired a tall, forked staff known as a "thumb stick." Some people saw it as an affectation or a symbol of authority, but Mead needed the staff for support.

Mead prided herself on her energy, work ethic, and ability to juggle multiple roles. As she sometimes told her hosts when visiting a campus or an institute, she wanted a full schedule in order to be "used" productively. Mead was driven, waking up at dawn if not earlier, and working at an almost frantic pace even as she entered her seventh decade. Her calendar was planned at least a year in advance, and she was always in demand. Wherever she went, Mead was recognized and admired, often being asked for an autograph, a media interview, or an impromptu class visit.

Mead continued to rely on her entourage to organize and manage her hectic schedule. Apart from regular secretarial assistance at the museum, she had assistants arranging appearances, checking mail, filing documents, grading student papers, and providing her with transportation, lodging, food, and drink. Some were former or current students; some were compensated, and others not. Rhoda Métraux, now her life partner and housemate, edited and coauthored many of Mead's publications, often without acknowledgment.

Mead was not necessarily an easy person to work for or with. She could be gracious, caring, and helpful, using her broad network to find employment for those close to her. But she could also be demanding, abrasive, judgmental, hostile, and hurtful. Mead was sometimes short-tempered. Some of her assistants simply quit, while others remained intensely loyal and respected Mead regardless (Grinager 1999: 262). Without this support system, Mead would have been unable to be in near-constant motion.

Mead's base of operations was a garret, a corner tower of the American Museum of Natural History. Here Mead continued her curatorial duties, providing the museum with over three thousand items for its collections, supervising displays and dioramas, raising (and contributing) funds, and overseeing the opening of the Hall of Pacific Peoples that now bears her name.

Mead became an adjunct professor at Columbia in 1954. Although not a regular faculty member, she was sought after by undergraduates, and, because Mead was spending more time in New York, she could now mentor more graduate students, especially women. Yet Mead was not necessarily appreciated by her academic colleagues, who considered her too "popular" and no longer engaged in cutting edge research. As Sydel Silverman, who entered the graduate program at Columbia in the late 1950s, recalled,

> My cohort was advised by more advanced graduate students to avoid working too closely with her; if you became her student you would have her attention and loyalty, but other professors would not take you seriously. Still, we took her courses and learned some useful things from her: how to pay attention, with an anthropological ear, to the world beyond the university; how to take field notes . . . and other wisdom, both valuable and dubious. (2004: 215)

Mead also taught at Yale, Emory, Vassar, Fordham, and New York University, among others, on visiting appointments. In addition, she was awarded honorary degrees by over two dozen colleges and universities, while extending her influence into many nonacademic realms.

LEADERSHIP AND ACTIVISM

Most academics would be content with recognition of their work by their peers, publication by prestigious academic presses, and invitations to speak at major institutions and conferences. Not so

Margaret Mead. She was much more than a well-known scholar and symbolic figurehead within her discipline; she was a leader in many organizations, large and small, both inside and outside of anthropology. In 1960 she became president of the American Anthropological Association, only the third woman to do so, and in 1974 she was elected president of the American Association for the Advancement of Science, only the second woman to be so honored. Mead was also president of the Society for Applied Anthropology, the Society for General Systems Research, the World Foundation for Mental Health, the Scientists' Institute for Public Information, and the World Society for Ekistics. She was an Episcopalian delegate to the World Council of Churches, founder of the Institute for Intercultural Studies, cofounder of the Human Lactation Center, and cofounder of the Delos Symposium.

As an activist, Mead's interests were eclectic, including urban planning, housing, the environment, nuclear war, the future, and race, as well as women, childhood, adolescence, aging, families, sex, marriage, and education. As evident in *Coming of Age in Samoa* and *Growing Up in New Guinea*, education had long been one of Mead's interests. She continued to publish a large number of articles on education and a major work on *The School in American Culture* (1951b) for professional educators. She also authored two children's books, including *An Interview with Santa Claus* (1978). On a practical level, Mead was involved with the progressive Downtown Community School in New York and, in the final year of her life, was president of the board of the Storefront Community School for disadvantaged children in East Harlem.

Mead loved to organize and attend small conferences where experts from different fields could interact, get to know each other, and delve into pressing issues (Mead and Byers 1978). In 1975, she organized one such conference on "The Atmosphere: Endangered and Endangering," in which participants learned about climate change well before it was recognized as an existential threat to the planet. Long after Mead's death, conservatives who did not concur with the scientific consensus on climate change discovered this little-known conference and demonized Mead as responsible for the so-called "global warming hoax," although Mead had simply organized the conference with no particular agenda in mind.

Mead continued her interest in psychoanalysis, an interest reciprocated by psychiatrists who valued her insights. She became a visiting professor of psychiatry at the University of Cincinnati Medical School and was a regular lecturer at the Menninger Foundation, as well as a member of the foundation's board of trustees. Although Mead was never analyzed, she did take Rorschach tests herself and had her dreams reviewed by analysts. Less conspicuously, Mead was also interested in astrology, parapsychology, and psychics; she personally used healers for illness in the final years of her life. And in keeping with her interest in human potentials, she was a close friend of Jean Houston, a leader of the Human Potential movement.

GOVERNMENT, CONGRESS, AND PRESIDENTS

Building on her experience with the U.S. government during and shortly after World War II, Mead became a regular presence in Washington, DC, as an activist. She followed issues of concern to her and met with government officials, sometimes at her request, being well connected to a large network of policy makers. For example, in 1976 she asked for a meeting with the head of the Department of Health, Education, and Welfare (HEW) because the National Institute for Mental Health's predoctoral research program had been canceled. Mead wanted this program reinstated because she felt it was essential for professional training. She got the meeting, during which she addressed the need for the predoctoral research program, as well as recommended participation by anthropologists on HEW panels and the employment of anthropologists in government research positions involving health care (Dillon 1981).

Mead often gave testimony as an activist and witness before U.S. congressional committees on a variety of subjects, including nuclear reactors, marijuana, the use of behavioral sciences in foreign policy, family structures, renewal of funding for the National

Science Foundation, the establishment of a National Anthropological Film Center at the Smithsonian, U.S. participation in the
United Nations, and recombinant DNA. She published work on
education for the Department of Health, Education, and Welfare
and edited a volume on cultural and technological change for the
United Nations Educational, Scientific, and Cultural Organization (1955). Some critics felt that Mead was addressing subjects
about which she knew very little and that she was spreading herself too thin. Yet Mead had great confidence in her views, a desire to make a difference, and an optimism about what she could
achieve.

Mead's fame and reputation gave her connections to American presidents and their spouses. She corresponded with Eleanor Roosevelt and the Kennedys, was an advisor on women's
issues to President Johnson, and was an advisor to President Carter. Mead supported Carter's presidential candidacy in 1976, corresponding with him as "Jimmy" and offering him advice about
his policies. Just before her death in 1978, Mead sent Carter an
urgent message from her hospital bed asking him not to veto the
Child Nutrition Act, which he was about to do. Instead, he approved the act and sent her a personal thank-you note. Mead also
met, interviewed, and corresponded with First Lady Rosalynn
Carter, who would sit in the front row of mourners at Mead's me-
morial service at the National Cathedral in Washington, DC.

A POLITICAL BALANCING ACT

Although Mead was involved with a number of political figures,
she nevertheless tried to remain nonpartisan when it came to
party politics. Her support for Carter in 1976 was the first and
only time that she publicly endorsed a presidential candidate.
While Mead had a reputation as a political liberal and was certainly able to speak her mind on many different issues, she did
not always do so even when she could. This can be seen in the
monthly columns for *Redbook* magazine that she authored from
1962 to 1978. For most of two decades, *Redbook* was Mead's most

durable and important public forum, with a readership of millions of young women. It was the most politically liberal of the several women's magazines of that period, and its editors did not shy away from controversial issues. Yet during the 1960s, Mead seemed to tiptoe around a number of these topics.

For example, although Mead had written about the Kennedys as public figures and authored a column about a new role for Jacqueline Kennedy after the assassination of President Kennedy in 1963, she did not address the assassination itself until 1965, when she was asked in a question-and-answer column whether there was a conspiracy to kill Kennedy. In that column, she discussed the differences between right-wing and left-wing conspiracy theories, saying almost nothing about Kennedy or the assassination itself.

The assassination was the most important event of 1963; it occurred during the American Anthropological Association meetings that Mead was attending in San Francisco. Many attendees were in a state of shock and disbelief as meeting sessions were interrupted with the announcement that the president had been shot. A number of anthropologists wanted to cancel sessions scheduled for later that day; Mead and others wanted to continue the afternoon sessions. Her recommendation to her colleagues was that they gather data on the public's reaction to the assassination (Howard 1984: 283n).

The assassinations of Martin Luther King Jr. and Robert F. Kennedy in 1968 also went unmentioned in Mead's *Redbook* columns, although Mead had briefly noted her admiration for King in an earlier column. The civil rights movement received little attention from Mead until 1969; absent, too, were the urban riots of the 1960s that shook Detroit, Newark, Los Angeles, New Haven, and other American cities. And the most divisive issue of that period—the Vietnam War—was also largely missing from Mead's columns in *Redbook* until 1970, long after President Johnson had decided not to run for reelection because of the war and after the tide of public opinion had turned against the war. Nevertheless, in 1970 Mead did make her vigorous opposition to the war known in a *Redbook* column, stating that the war had been a "gross mistake" from the beginning. And she would advocate for American withdrawal from Vietnam in public testimony before the Senate Foreign Relations Committee.

THE THAILAND CONTROVERSY[1]

In the early 1970s, an issue related to the Vietnam war landed squarely in Mead's lap when she became involved in a major controversy within anthropology. In 1970, at the height of the anti-war movement, a student research assistant employed by anthropologist Michael Moerman at UCLA obtained documents from his files that seemed to demonstrate that four anthropologists and other academics were working for a U.S. government military agency involved in secret counterinsurgency programs in Thailand. Some of the documents were then published in the *Student Mobilizer*, an "underground" newspaper of the Student Mobilization Committee to End the War in Vietnam. These revelations led to an exposé in the prestigious *New York Review of Books* by two members of the Ethics Committee of the American Anthropological Association (AAA) who were deeply concerned that Thai peasants were being placed in harm's way. Moreover, the counterinsurgency programs' goals appeared to be a clear violation of the AAA code of ethics. The accused responded that their work was not secret or controversial and that their reputations had been tarnished by unethical colleagues in the AAA.

As a result of the controversy over these programs, the association formed a special committee to investigate the matter with Mead as its chair. Because of her experience in government during World War II, Mead was aware of the issues involved in classified national security work, and she was expected to be an effective arbiter. The investigative committee, known as the Mead Committee, consisted of three anthropologists, who poured over several thousand pages of documents and solicited information from a variety of sources.

The issues were complex, involving American anthropologists, Australian anthropologists, Thai hill tribes, the Thai military, communist insurgents, and American military interests. Focusing on the specific allegations against the four anthropologists, the Mead Committee concluded that the charges were less substantial than they appeared. The committee found that the allegedly unethical activities were well within the bounds of acceptable professional behavior and not unusual for applied anthropologists. It also reported that the accused anthropologists had contributed much of value to anthropology. Furthermore, the committee was critical of the AAA Ethics Committee members who initially reviewed the documents and published allegations about the accused. The committee did note that there was the larger ethical issue concerning the possibility that routine ethnographic data gathered and published by anthropologists could be used by governments against those studied; however, they believed that this was an issue for future consideration and not directly relevant to the committee's findings.

The Mead Report was issued just prior to the 1971 annual meetings of the American Anthropological Association, so the membership had little opportunity to examine its contents. Nevertheless, the report was the subject of a lengthy debate and a vote at the meetings. During a heated four-hour evening session with an initial audience of about seven hundred, members passionately defended or disagreed with the report's conclusions. To many younger members of the association, the report seemed like a whitewash. Mead was actually hissed at and booed by some in the audience. The well-organized radical caucus was particularly vocal in its objections. Some speakers argued that the real issue was the war in Vietnam and that a vote against the report was a vote against the war. As the meeting continued past midnight, most members retired to their hotel rooms. When a vote was finally taken, the report was overwhelmingly rejected.

In the wake of the controversy, a number of young anthropologists continued to be critical of Mead. She resented their criticism, having worked with committee members to support the report's specific conclusions and having taken a public anti-Vietnam war stand. Mead and her fellow committee members, who had initially sought to preserve all of the documents they reviewed, decided to destroy them instead, fearing they might be misused in further political infighting among different factions of the association. The Thailand controversy accentuated divisions within the association, left Mead furious, and has remained contentious (Hinton 2002; Jonsson 2014; Petersen 2015).

AN AGENT OF EMPIRE?

Concern about the possible misuse of anthropological research also led to a critical look at past work by Mead and other foundational figures in the discipline. Critics Angela Gilliam and Lenora Foerstel linked Mead's earlier work to colonial and imperial interests, including the charge that she had a "deep commitment to Westernization and laissez faire capitalism" (1992: 145). While Mead did conduct fieldwork in three colonial territories, she did not collaborate with the American, Australian, and Dutch regimes. She was not an apologist for or an agent of empire, nor were most anthropologists of her generation (H. Lewis 2014). Mead supported decolonization and urged a "wariness of neocolonialism" (1975: 434). Indeed, the people of Pere appreciated her interventions with Australian administrators on their behalf. Moreover, with the exception of World War II, Mead was not a partner of the American military, nor did she support American military engagements in the 1960s, such as the Bay of Pigs invasion and the Vietnam war. Rather, she supported a number of liberal political causes, including world peace, denuclearization, and environmental protection.

In terms of America's role in the world, Mead was a globalist. In 1965, she wrote:

As a people, it has taken us almost four centuries to weld ourselves into what is now—almost—a united nation. Much of what we have accomplished has come about through the pressures of the outside world. Strong, wealthy, and powerful, we must now turn toward the rest of the world ready to accept a responsibility that is bound not to the duties, the

loyalties, and the hopes of earlier years, but to the whole
world, the only world in which we can act today and carry
out our highest hopes for the future. We have no other.
(Mead [l965a] 2000: 197)

Micaela di Leonardo, also a critic of Mead, has found this kind
of thinking "imperializing, condescending and prescriptive"
(1998: 343). Yet Mead's "imperializing" was more liberal than
imperial. She privately criticized colonial administrators in New
Guinea and deplored the treatment of Native Americans based
on her work with the Omaha. Mead was proud that anthropologists "valued what others undervalued," and believed that her
colleagues were "champions of the dispossessed, defenders of
the despised and neglected, [and] pleaders for a wider view and
a greater tolerance" (1975: 427). She was also a supporter of the
United Nations and worried about the unintended consequences
of modernization, urbanization, and development, expressing
her concerns in *World Enough: Rethinking the Future* (Mead and
Heyman 1960).

THE AMERICAN FUTURE

In the late 1960s and early 1970s—the Nixon era prior to Water-
gate—Mead's hope for America's future was challenged by political schisms and a lack of confidence in government and public
officials. Although her reputation within anthropology had di-
minished as a result of the Thailand controversy, in this fraught
political environment the public largely saw Mead as a trusted
figure. Indeed, in 1972 there was even a small movement promoting "Margaret Mead for President." She politely declined, believing that she could be more effective in a nonpartisan capacity.

During this period, the Vietnam War, the racial divide, and
the "generation gap" led younger Americans to wonder whether
there were viable solutions to any of these issues. Viewing herself as a mediator across generations, Mead sought to bridge this
chasm and, when possible, promote guarded optimism about

the future. She acknowledged that for young people the future seemed bleak. In *Culture and Commitment* (1970), a popular book addressing the generation gap, Mead posed the question asked by young Americans: "*Is there anything in human cultures as they exist today worth saving, worth committing my life to?*" (1970: xii, her italics). In response, Mead summarized what she learned from her fieldwork experiences, hoping that they might provide a guide to the future. She distinguished between three kinds of cultures: those in which children learned primarily from adults, those in which children and adults learned from their peers, and those in which adults also learned from their children. Mead pinned her hopes on these latter cultures, advocating a future in which young people could play a more active role, making positive contributions for all humanity.

Mead's desire for a better future was also evident in her conversation about race with the noted author and civil rights activist James Baldwin. This issue had great importance and immediacy during 1960s and early 1970s, with Baldwin as one of the most articulate voices of the Black protest. Mead, approaching seventy and less involved with race, considered herself a voice of reason on this issue, just as she had been on the generation gap. The two met for a weekend dialogue lasting over seven hours that was then condensed and broadcast on national television. Their dialogue was also transformed into a coauthored book, *A Rap on Race* (1971).

Based on his experiences as an "exile," Baldwin despaired of the racial divisions that plagued America, stating that his hope for the future had been dashed by lies and betrayals. He held current American citizens responsible for past injustices, while Mead held them accountable only for present and future injustices. In sometimes tense exchanges, Mead encouraged Baldwin not to think of himself as a victim and to embrace hope. A number of people felt that Mead's optimism was naïve and that she did not fully appreciate where Baldwin and Black Americans were coming from. However, Mead had a record of support for racial equality, dating back to her critique of racial thinking in her master's thesis in psychology. She strongly endorsed human rights efforts, refused to speak at segregated colleges, and helped create a model integrated school in New York City a decade before the Supreme Court ordered desegregation in 1954 (Yans 2004: 244). Available on the internet, the Mead-Baldwin dialogue continues to draw strong and contrasting reactions, as well as offering still another window on Mead's complex political persona.

NOTE

1. On the Thailand controversy, see Price (2016), Wakin (1992), Hinton (2002), Jonsson (2014), and Petersen (2015).

CHAPTER 10

WOMEN'S ISSUES AND THE *REDBOOK* COLUMNS

● ● ●

As mentioned, in the 1960s and 1970s Mead's most important and influential public forum was her monthly column for *Redbook*, the long-established, mainstream women's magazine with a progressive bent on social and political issues. Readers were young, middle-class women, often married, and more educated than the stereotypical "women's magazine" reader. *Redbook* had a growing audience of three million subscribers in the 1960s, expanding to five million in the 1970s. In 1962, with Rhoda Métraux as her silent coauthor, Mead began writing these columns and continued to do so for the next seventeen years, authoring almost two hundred columns in all. No other anthropologist and very few writers of any stripe have had this kind of extended public forum.

The *Redbook* columns comprised a substantial portion of Mead's publications for this period, including her academic publications. In previous decades, she had already written a good deal about women, mothers, marriage, families, and sex, drawing public praise as well as criticism. The 1960s, though, proved particularly challenging because the decade was a time of major change for American women and men, including the beginning of the sexual revolution and the second wave of the women's movement. How would Mead approach women's issues in this rapidly evolving social environment?

On some issues, Mead was ahead of public opinion. She approved of abortion as a necessary choice and disapproved of laws against homosexuality because they attempted to control private behavior. However, on other issues such as coeducation, Mead was hardly liberal. She opposed coeducation—that is, men and women attending the same college. And she did not think that college was as necessary for young women as it was for men.

During the first half of the 1960s, Mead actively discouraged premarital sex, promoted stay-at-home motherhood, neglected the systematic discrimination against women in the workforce, and worried about the "feminization" of men. Nor did she support the Equal Rights Amendment, fearing that it would hurt women who were already mothers and homemakers, as well as harming relationships between men and women.

SEX AND MARRIAGE

As an example of Mead's thinking in the early 1960s, consider her *Redbook* columns on premarital sex. In 1962, Mead encouraged young women to "keep sex where it belongs"—within the institution of marriage. She warned that "during engagement, the modern girl is often dangerously relaxed" about sex. As for her future husband, he "must protect his future marriage from premature paternity." For Mead, marriage was too important to be compromised by premarital sex. In a *Redbook* column addressing "Sex on Campus: The Real Issue" (October 1962), Mead agreed with the president of Vassar who had also spoken against premarital sex.

Mead did allow that "premarital sex is alright provided that it ends in marriage" and that pregnancy could be rewarded when "the girl gets her man." But she encouraged single women to take advantage of the "opportunity" to "remain single and abstinent and responsible." Within marriage, Mead stated that a wife must satisfy her husband so that he would never look at another woman; she felt that it was primarily a woman's responsibility to prevent the twin threats of premarital and extramarital sex. Public opinion polls from this period suggest that these opinions were consistent with ideas and behaviors held by most American women at the time.

As the 1960s progressed, Mead's views on these issues required some modification. In 1966, she acknowledged that marriage was occurring later, that postponing sex into one's mid-twenties was "unfair and unreasonable," and that the "double standard" no longer held. These trends concerned Mead not because she wished to encourage young women to engage in premarital sex or postpone marriage, but because she saw these practices as eroding the prevailing consensus about the value of premarital chastity and the importance of marriage itself.

To save the institution of marriage and encourage sex within marriage, Mead offered her *Redbook* readers a proposal for two types (or two "steps") of legal marriage (July 1966). The first type was individual marriage, which would be childless, easy to enter, and easy to end. The second type was parental marriage, which would be harder to enter because the economic means to support a child would be a prerequisite, and would be harder to dissolve because children were involved. These two types of marriage would, first, "dignify" early sexual relationships and, second, spell out the responsibilities necessary to strengthen parenthood. Mead emphasized that this was merely a contribution to a discussion of issues confronting the modern family, not a policy to be enacted. Nevertheless, there was a backlash.

According to Mead, readers responded vigorously, stating that, "sex is not a shoe to be tried on." Experts replied that "marriage is yes or no, not maybe." And students asked, "Why get married at all?" Two years later Mead replied with a column titled "A Continuing Dialogue on Marriage: Why Just 'Living Together' Won't Work" (April 1968). Noting that fundamental changes in society had taken place, Mead apologized to readers for the manner in which she had proposed her two types of marriage, admitting, "I know now that some of the things were wrong in the way I presented my proposal." She reported that attitudes toward contraception were changing rapidly, that sex was not intrinsically wrong, and that young people wanted "sex freedom." However, Mead maintained a resolute legal posture, warning that "living together ... *is* against the law" and could lead to blackmail, exposure, public penalties, expulsion from college, and "disgrace and damaged careers." In addition, she noted that people still thought that living together was "sinful."

Mead concluded that laws must be changed but that "living together" outside the bonds of marriage was "law breaking." And this kind of law breaking was being done by the "best" elements of society—that is, by middle- and upper-class young people. Mead expressed her concern that this trend could "bring down the whole social order." She then issued an emphatic marry-or-else statement, declaring, "If you want full-time companionship with someone you love . . . you had better get legally married, use contraceptives responsibly, and risk divorce later. You are risking even more if you don't."

THE STATUS OF WOMEN

In writing about women's issues, Mead was more than a magazine columnist. She played an active role in shaping public opinion beyond her *Redbook* columns. In the early 1960s, she had been invited to lead the Department of Health, Education, and Welfare (*Redbook*, February 1964) and would become an advisor to President Johnson on women's issues. In November of 1963, Mead devoted a column to *The President's Commission on the Status of Women* (1963), a report initiated by President Kennedy that was perhaps the definitive document on women's status during this period. Summarizing some of the commission's findings, Mead noted that by 1963, one in three married women were working and that eight in ten would work at some point during their lives. More women were entering the workforce, including young mothers, and the economy was coming to rely on the two-income household rather than the conventional male-breadwinner household. Although Mead did not discuss discrimination against women in her column, the commission report directly addressed this issue and recommended better working conditions, equal opportunities for women, maternity leave, and fairer allowances for divorce and widowhood, along with many other recommendations. The commission distributed a large run of eighty thousand copies of the report within a year.

In 1965, a commercial edition of *The President's Commission on the Status of Women*, titled *American Women*, was published by Charles Scribner's Sons and sold extremely well (Coontz 2011: 152). Although Mead had not been a member of the original Presidential Commission, she did coedit *American Women*, as well as authored its introduction and epilogue (Mead and Balgley 1965). While the body of *American Women* reported on pervasive forms of discrimination against women as a central finding, just as the original report had, Mead did not discuss discrimination against women in her introduction or in her epilogue. Instead, she focused on the dilemmas of women trying to balance their traditional roles as wives, homemakers, and mothers with their new roles in the workforce.

In January 1962, Mead wrote that college-educated women wanted to marry, stay home, and have children. In 1963, she noted that while women were entering the workforce, men needed careers; women did not. Mead thought that women should have a choice between staying at home and working. Her 1963 column on the *President's Commission on the Status of Women* was titled, "Do We Undervalue Full-Time Wives?," observing that *someone* had to stay home with the children. The following month, in December of 1963, Mead was asked about the status of women in the Soviet Union. She responded that due to a workforce deficit as the result of World War II, Soviet women had filled gaps in the workplace left by men, but that while more Soviet women were employed and in better positions than women in the United States, there were problems that resulted from women's participation in the Soviet workplace, noting that America "protects men's sense of masculinity by keeping women out" of the workforce.

In April of 1964, the question of Mead's own career was raised by a reader who asked Mead about the seeming contradiction between her recommendation that women should be responsible for full-time childcare and Mead's own life, in which she continued to work while others raised her daughter, Cathy. Mead responded by noting her own background and her mother's way of performing "small jobs that only a woman can do." Mead also replied that World War II required her to work for the war effort, and that childcare by others was acceptable in her "composite" household, although "the importance of mother love" could not be underestimated.

For Mead, there was no contradiction between her own life and her belief in appropriate women's roles. She cited the president's wife, Mrs. Lyndon Baines Johnson, as representing her conception of "total womanliness," a woman who was both at home in the White House and active in the world, working with volunteer organizations and children, as well as working against racial discrimination in the South (*Redbook*, July 1965). Later that year, Mead answered a related question about whether a woman could be fulfilled without work outside the home. She noted that caring for others was feminine—indeed part of the "feminine arts"—and that traditionally there was "lasting contentment" linked to being a wife and mother. Previously, the norm was that "the identity of a married woman . . . is defined by who her husband is and what he does. Today . . . this is no longer true" (November 1965).

The change in women's roles from home-based wife and mother to working mother was not always positive, according to Mead, who was concerned about the "defeminization" of women's "maternal humanizing role" due to early marriage, acceptance of the supermom myth, and a standard of living that now required women to work. She also found it dehumanizing to encourage women to enter into aggressive and competitive behaviors typical of men (March 1966). Her hope was that women and men would learn to cooperate in the future (January 1968) to a point where men entered "feminine" occupations and where both men and women would collaborate in "homemaking," bringing this previously feminine role "greater dignity" (March 1968). It was not until a column in 1970 that Mead would write about systematic discrimination against women in its many forms.

In a related column, Mead pointedly criticized the women's liberation movement, stating that the "shock tactics" of Women's Lib were leading to a "crisis" (June 1970). She had previously rebuked many unnamed feminists whom she characterized as "angry, bitter, and violent" (March 1970). According to Mead, these "stormy and obstreperous radicals" were "conspicuously self-centered and hostile women" that should not be allowed to "take over." For her, the differences between men and women needed recognition, not revolution. For Mead, men's strengths were mastery, exploration, and rational objectivity; women's strengths were being people-oriented, being subjective, having intimacy of understanding, and being caregivers.

Clearly Mead was not in the vanguard of the women's movement, although she was considered an ally of the movement. Her *Redbook* columns of the 1960s do not reflect the Margaret Mead who, in *Coming of Age in Samoa, Growing Up in New Guinea,* and *Sex and Temperament in Three Primitive Societies,* had significantly altered public understanding of adolescence, childhood, and gender roles. Like *Male and Female,* these columns reveal a Mead less inclined to push the envelope of public opinion and more likely to conform to it (Janiewski 2001). And, as in many of her roles in the latter part of her life, Mead was less an anthropologist and more a public intellectual. The *Redbook* columns contain relatively little anthropology and relatively little mention of other anthropologists, even those such as Jules Henry, who wrote a bestseller about America in *Culture against Man* (1963).

As noted, the views Mead expressed in her *Redbook* columns were often at odds with the life that Mead herself had led both privately and as a career woman. Indeed, she was criticized by feminists of the period for reinforcing a largely reproductive and domestic role for women—a traditional view that prevented women's realization of their full potential, something that Mead had advocated elsewhere. She also kept her views about free love and her bisexual life private, fearing public exposure and possible scandal.

The actual content of Mead's *Redbook* columns of this period may alter the common perception of Mead as a leader of the women's movement and an advocate for the sexual revolution. Nevertheless, her influence on women during this period cannot be underestimated. Betty Friedan, a prominent feminist and a critic of Mead, stated this unequivocally:

The most powerful influence on modern women, in terms of both functionalism and the feminist protest was Margaret Mead. Her work on culture and personality—book after book, study after study—has had a profound effect on the women of my generation, the one before it, and the generation now growing up. She was, and still is, the symbol of the woman thinker in America. She has written millions of words in the thirty-odd years between *Coming of Age in Samoa* and her latest article on American women in the *New York Times Magazine* or *Redbook*. She is studied in college classrooms by girls taking courses in anthropology, sociology, psychology, education, and marriage and family life; in graduate schools by those who will one day teach girls and counsel women; in medical schools by future pediatricians and psychiatrists; even in theological schools by progressive young ministers. And she is read in the women's magazines and the Sunday supplements, where she publishes as regularly as in the learned journals, by girls and women of all ages—and her influence has been felt in almost every layer of American thought. (1963: 126–127)

In Freidan's view, Mead not only spoke to young women, she spoke for them.

As the 1960s and 1970s progressed, Mead did alter a number of her positions, including those on discrimination against women, the Equal Rights Amendment, and the sexual revolution. In 1974, she authored a *Redbook* column on bisexuality as a human potential. And Mead was increasingly vocal about overpopulation, the destruction of the environment, and threat of war.

NOTE

On Mead's *Redbook* columns, see Shankman (2018b), from which much of this chapter is taken.

CHAPTER 11

THE MEAD-FREEMAN CONTROVERSY

• • •

When Mead died in 1978, her passing was recognized as a major event. In death she became something more than a public figure—a legend of sorts. However, five years later, in January 1983, her legendary status was questioned in a news story that appeared on the front page of the *New York Times*. It bore the headline "New Samoa Book Challenges Margaret Mead's Conclusions" and set off a firestorm of academic and public controversy lasting to the present.

The *Times* was reporting on Derek Freeman's *Margaret Mead and Samoa: The Making and Unmaking of an Anthropological Myth* (1983), a critical analysis of *Coming of Age in Samoa* that was published by the prestigious Harvard University Press. Freeman, a relatively unknown senior anthropologist at the Australian National University, was an expert on Samoan culture, having done research in Western Samoa (now independent Samoa) in the 1940s and 1960s. Although his book was academic in nature with much detail about Samoan custom, it had a message that resonated far beyond the groves of academe: Margaret Mead was wrong! In Freeman's view, he had "staggered the establishment."

Freeman gave Mead's book exceptional significance, contending that *Coming of Age in Samoa* was the cornerstone of twentieth-century cultural anthropology and American intellectual thought more generally. Mead herself made no such claims. Although popular and influential in the public realm, *Coming of*

Age in Samoa was not a foundational text for anthropologists. Freeman simply confused the book's popularity with its professional credibility.

THE ISSUES

Freeman argued that Samoans were puritanical and sexually restrictive rather than sexually permissive, as Mead had described them. Samoa was not a tropical paradise with islanders engaging in casual sex under the palms; instead, it was a sexually repressive culture in which virginity was more highly valued than perhaps any other culture known to anthropology. In contrast to Mead's portrayal of a relatively conflict-free adolescence, Freeman contended that Samoan adolescence was a time of "storm and stress," riddled with conflict, aggression, and rape. He stated his case with great authority and what seemed to be an overwhelming amount of evidence. His Samoa and Mead's Samoa were like night and day.

Beyond the details of Samoan adolescence, for Freeman there was the broader nature-nurture controversy and whether Mead's emphasis on the importance of culture, as opposed to biology, was warranted. Freeman labeled Mead an "absolute cultural determinist" who allowed no role for biology whatsoever. But Samoa and even the nature-nurture controversy were not what attracted most readers' attention to the *Times* story. *Coming of Age in Samoa* had established Mead's reputation and was a significant part of her legacy for the public. Freeman's critique had the potential to severely damage that reputation, transforming her image from trusted public figure to cultural roadkill. This was news.

Although there had been criticism of *Coming of Age in Samoa* since its publication in 1928, including criticism by Samoans, during her lifetime Mead was able to respond in new prefaces as the book was republished in subsequent decades. But because she had died five years before *Margaret Mead and Samoa* was published, Mead was unable to personally reply to Freeman's critique. There would be no public debate between Mead and Freeman. However, there was controversy because *Margaret Mead and Samoa: The Making and Unmaking of an Anthropological Myth* was about the unmaking of one of anthropology's almost mythical figures—Mead herself.

The story in the *Times* became the opening salvo in the longest and most acrimonious controversy in the history of cultural anthropology. A virtual avalanche of media coverage followed, as did professional meetings, articles, books, films, and plays about the controversy. Freeman came to the United States in 1983 on a publicity tour for his book, appearing on multiple radio programs and television shows, including a full-hour network television appearance on the very popular *Donahue* show viewed by an audience of millions.

THE CULTURE WARS

Freeman's critique also reflected the larger "culture wars" raging within American society in the 1980s. Conservatives viewed Mead as a liberal, a feminist, and a woman who advocated the allegedly false doctrine of cultural relativism. For them, Freeman's work showed that Mead was not only wrong about Samoa, but that she had recklessly promoted sexual permissiveness and in doing so caused lasting moral damage to American youth. In the words of philosopher and critic Allan Bloom, Mead was a "sexual adventurer" (1987: 33). Moreover, after the American Anthropological Association passed a motion criticizing Freeman's book, conservatives came to see anthropologists as apologists for Mead and cut from the same liberal cloth. Thus, Mead and anthropology became lightning rods in the culture wars.

Because his home was in Australia, Freeman was initially unaware of how his arguments were being used in the American culture wars, but he soon realized that he had allies in his critique of Mead and welcomed them. Even as Freeman was losing support among American anthropologists, he was gaining support in the wider court of public opinion.

The controversy was accessible to the public as a story about Mead's fall from grace. At the same time, it was so ethnographically and historically complex that anthropologists had difficulty resolving it. On one level, the controversy seemed to be a "he said, she said" affair. Freeman was a male, originally from New Zealand, who worked in Western Samoa in the 1940s and 1960s, primarily with Samoan males. Mead was an American woman who worked in a different Samoa—American Samoa—in the 1920s, primarily with adolescent girls. So, of course, they might have differing views of Samoan culture. Yet there were factual issues in the controversy where evidence would prove decisive.

VIRGINITY

Freeman portrayed Samoa as a culture in which virginity was highly valued as an ideal for all girls as exemplified by the role of the *taupou*, or ceremonial virgin, whose public defloration preceded her marriage to a high-ranking chief or heir apparent to a high title. Such marriages cemented political alliances. While this dramatic demonstration of the *taupou*'s virginity occurred before and during the early missionization of the islands in the nineteenth century, at the time of Mead's fieldwork in the 1920s, she noted that the role of the *taupou* was far less important than it had been prior to missionization and that the public defloration ceremony had been abolished. With political alliances no longer vital, the *taupou* system of marriage was in marked decline.

In his unpublished work, Freeman himself reported that the *taupou* system in Western Samoa was, in his words, "virtually defunct" (1948: 245), just as it was in American Samoa. And he offered a detailed account of why it was no longer important. In other words, Freeman knew from his own research and decades before his published critique of Mead that she and other scholars were accurate on this point. However, neglecting that research, he took the role of the *taupou* out of its historical context and gave it a significance it no longer had. Mead herself had warned against confusing the past with the present in *Coming of Age in Samoa* ([1928b] 1973: 273).

Freeman also stated that Samoans valued female virginity "to a greater extreme than perhaps in any other culture known to anthropology" (1983: 250), emphasizing Samoan public ideology. In Samoan belief and especially among high-ranking families, virginity was highly valued. But did this sincerely held belief translate into actual conduct? In practice, Mead found that over 40 percent of the twenty-five adolescent girls in her sample were sexually active before marriage, becoming active a few years after puberty. The older the girls, the more likely they were to engage in sexual activity. She also found that girls who resided in the pastor's home were less likely to engage in sexual activity.

Freeman's own data on sexual conduct reveal the same trend—the older the girls, the more likely they were to be sexually active. In addition, Freeman found that lower-ranking girls were more likely to be sexually active than girls from higher-ranking families. So while virginity was highly prized as an ideal, it was not necessarily mirrored in private conduct. More generally, cross-cultural research about the value placed on virginity indicates that the Samoans were less restrictive than Freeman argued, although not as permissive as Mead suggested (Schlegel 1991).

Freeman first visited Western Samoa in the early 1940s as a schoolteacher. He was in the islands when World War II broke out in the Pacific and as tens of thousands of American servicemen arrived in Western Samoa in preparation for combat in the western Pacific. Interethnic unions between these servicemen and unmarried Samoan women were common, with a number of children resulting from these unions. Had Samoa been a sexually restrictive culture, young women would have been secluded from contact with servicemen, forbidden from having affairs, and punished for doing so. Samoan families would have strongly objected to such unions and would have had antagonistic relationships with servicemen and their officers. But this was not the case. These unions were open, allowed, and approved by Samoan families; conflicts with servicemen were rare, and offspring were generally welcomed. Since Freeman was in Western Samoa during much of the war, he was a position to have known of these unions, but in his extensive writing about Samoan sexual conduct they go unmentioned (Shankman 1996).

NATURE AND NURTURE

On the issue of adolescent storm and stress, Freeman emphasized the presence of conflict, rivalry, aggression, and rape, contending that Mead neglected these subjects. However, as illustrated in a chapter on "The Girl in Conflict" in *Coming of Age in Samoa*, Mead acknowledged adolescent stress, but argued that the lives of Samoan adolescent girls were *relatively* less stressful than the lives of American girls in the 1920s. Although this comparison was impressionistic rather than carefully documented, this was Mead's standard, one that Freeman did not address.

For Mead, the difference between Samoan and American adolescence was cultural, not biological. In *Coming of Age in Samoa*, Mead clearly stated that puberty was a universal biological process through which all young people passed, but how that process was managed and what adolescence meant in different cultures was variable. Cross-cultural research on adolescence (Schlegel and Barry 1991) and research on adolescence in Pacific Island cultures (Herdt and Leavitt 1998) have confirmed Mead's original observation about the variability of the adolescent experience. And, as evident in her work over several decades, Mead continually explored the interrelationship between culture and biology.

In framing the controversy in terms of nature versus nurture, Freeman tapped into an issue that was being hotly debated in scientific and cultural circles in the 1980s. In his view, Mead had tried to demonstrate that nature was unimportant and even irrelevant, a message that Freeman saw as having disastrous consequences for anthropology and the world at large. This supposedly anti-biological, anti-evolutionary, and anti-scientific perspective that Freeman attributed to Mead was a key component of his assault on her reputation and was for him the most significant and far-reaching consequence of what he called "Mead's mistake."

The nature-nurture dimension of the controversy also attracted a number of influential scholars to Freeman's cause. Mead
and Samoa became pawns in the intellectual struggle between
those who favored a more biologically oriented approach to human behavior and those who favored a more culturally oriented
approach. Intelligent people with an interest in biology, genetics,
sociobiology, and evolutionary psychology, including prominent
figures such as Steven Pinker, David Buss, and Matt Ridley, often
assumed that Freeman's argument about Mead was correct and
used it to condemn her with the same certainty that Freeman
brought to his critique.

Mead was vilified as a representative of the *tabula rasa* school
of human nature, in which individuals were regarded as blank
slates on which anything could be written. She was excoriated
as hopelessly lost to the archaic and misguided cause of cultural
determinism. Of course, there was nothing wrong in criticizing
Mead and *Coming of Age in Samoa*, but on the nature-nurture
issue her critics had embraced Freeman's allegations to such an
extent that they missed what Mead had actually written on this
subject and had presented in major addresses to the American
Anthropological Association (Mead 1961) and the American Association for the Advancement of Science (Mead 1976), in which
she highlighted the importance of evolution and genetics. Freeman's assertion that she was an "absolute cultural determinist"
was simply untrue.

THE "FATEFUL HOAXING" OF MARGARET MEAD

Freeman's critique of Mead continued in a second book, *The
Fateful Hoaxing of Margaret Mead: A Historical Analysis of Her
Samoan Research* (1999). Extending his argument that Mead was
wrong about the alleged sexual permissiveness of Samoan adolescent girls, Freeman addressed the only remaining question:
how could she have been so mistaken? Freeman hypothesized
that Mead must have been the unwitting victim of Samoan jok-
ing, a common practice among the islanders. According to Free-

man, Mead was a naïve young woman who embraced the cultural determinism of her mentor Franz Boas, who was unprepared for fieldwork, who did not do sufficient fieldwork, and who did not understand Samoan custom. Therefore, when she inquired about Samoan sexual conduct, Mead was unaware that Samoans were telling her innocent lies about their private lives that she believed as the truth and published as fact in *Coming of Age in Samoa*. In Freeman's words, Mead had been "fatefully" hoaxed, "completely" hoaxed, and "grossly" hoaxed.

The implication of the hoaxing argument for Mead's fieldwork competence was damning. What could be worse for an anthropologist than to be duped by one's own informants and collaborators? However, Freeman argued that Mead was not a deliberate cheat in portraying Samoan adolescents as sexually permissive; she was simply a foolish young woman who never realized the nature of her error. In making the argument that Mead was the unwitting victim of her own inexperience and preconceptions rather than a conscious perpetrator of ethnographic fraud, Freeman saw himself as salvaging Mead's reputation from certain ruin. He was absolving her of being a charlatan by finding that she was "in a state of cognitive delusion" (1991: 117), her "fateful hoaxing" the result of her own "self-deception." Indeed, in Freeman's opinion, "there isn't another example of such wholesale self-deception in the history of behavioral sciences" (McDowell 1990: 213). This "defense" of Mead was ingenious, but it assumed adequate support for the hoaxing argument in the first place.

To document the hypothesis that Mead had been hoaxed, Freeman did further research in the islands. In 1989, he reported that he had found a key witness to support the hoaxing argument, a Samoan woman who was allegedly Mead's "chief informant" and closest friend; her name was Fa'apua'a Fa'amū. Freeman stated that, in an interview with Fa'apua'a, she had confessed that she and her friend Fofoa responded to Mead's questions about what they did at night with innocent fibs, never realizing that their jokes would become the definitive word on Samoan sexual conduct. According to Freeman, Fa'apua'a had provided him with the missing link in his argument.

Furthermore, in his reconstruction of Mead's Samoan field-work, Freeman stated that he was able to trace the alleged hoax-ing to a precise date and time—the evening of 13 March 1926. For Freeman, this was the "only way" to explain Mead's portrayal of permissive Samoan sexual conduct, discounting her data on the twenty-five adolescent girls on whom she had detailed data, as well as her interviews with Samoan women and men. The in-terview with Fa'apua'a was the capstone of Freeman's critique of Mead—"smoking gun" evidence so convincing that he declared it could be presented "in a court of law." He had finally discov-ered, through patient scholarship, "the truth about what hap-pened." Fa'apua'a's testimony was of such "exceptional historical significance" that it "effectively solved" the problem of how Mead got Samoa wrong. For Freeman, "no sequence of events has had a greater effect on anthropology in the twentieth cen-tury" (1999: 27).

If true, Freeman's hoaxing argument represented an amazing feat of historical detective work. However, like much of Free-man's critique of Mead, it was untrue. Mead was nobody's fool. Additional research has demonstrated that Fa'apua'a was not a "chief informant" or any kind of informant for Mead on Samoan sexual conduct. Moreover, to understand Fa'apua'a's testimony and the context in which she gave it, it is necessary to review the complete transcripts of all three of Freeman's interviews with her, not just the brief excerpt from the first interview that Free-man quoted.

The full transcripts of the three interviews were never pub-lished; participants in the controversy simply assumed that Free-man had quoted and interpreted Fa'apua'a's testimony accurately and transparently. When Fa'apua'a stated that the two women joked about spending their nights "with boys," Freeman assumed that she quite literally meant that they, "along with other young women of Manu'a, were sexually promiscuous night after night with a succession of different young men" (Freeman 1989: 1020), and that this is what Mead believed.

Yet a thorough analysis of the transcripts shows that, accord-ing to Fa'apua'a herself, when asked *directly* about what she and

Fofoa discussed with Mead, Fa'apua'a responded emphatically that Mead did not ask the two women about their private lives. In subsequent interviews, Fa'apua'a also stated that Mead never asked her and Fofoa about the sexual conduct of adolescent girls, nor did they provide Mead with such information. How then could Mead have been hoaxed?

Freeman simply omitted those parts of the interviews with Fa'apua'a that were inconvenient to his argument and then misrepresented her testimony to anthropologists and the public. From the interviews, there is no compelling evidence that Mead was hoaxed or that Fa'apua'a and Fofoa misled Mead on adolescent sexual conduct (Shankman 2013).[1]

Had the complete interviews been available to interested researchers, the hoaxing argument would not have been credible. Challenged by multiple critics, including anthropologist Martin Orans (1999) and sociologist James Côté (2001), among others, Freeman dismissed them out of hand, labeling them "enemies," "adversaries," and "opponents."

During the last fifteen years of his life, Freeman used virtually all of his public presentations and writing to spread the tale of Mead's alleged hoaxing and his message that "Mead's mistake" had an enormous impact on the world at large. He declared:

> We are here dealing with one of the most spectacular events of the 20th century. Margaret Mead, as we know, was grossly hoaxed by her Samoan informants, and Mead in her turn, by convincing others of the "genuineness" of her account of Samoa, completely misinformed and misled virtually the entire anthropological establishment, as well as the intelligentsia at large . . . . That a Polynesian prank should have produced such a result is deeply comic. But behind the comedy there is a chastening reality. It is now apparent that for decade after decade in countless textbooks, and in university and college lecture rooms throughout the Western world, students were misinformed about an issue of fundamental importance by professors placing credence in Mead's conclusion of 1928 who had themselves become cognitively

deluded. Never can giggly fibs have had such far-reaching
consequences in the groves of academe. (1997: 68)

This was a good story, a story that people wanted to believe,
including a number of academics. Almost no one thought that it
might be necessary to review all three interviews with Fa'apua'a
and ask if Freeman had accurately represented her testimony. He
stated his argument with such authority and presented it with
such conviction that it seemed believable. In fact, it seemed foolish not to believe him. Alas, it was a story was too good to be
true.[2]

WHAT THE CONTROVERSY MEANT TO SAMOANS

How did Samoans respond to the controversy? The publication
of Freeman's critique of Mead encouraged a number of Samoans to offer their own views of *Coming of Age in Samoa*. As Mead
wrote her book, she thought about what her work might mean to
an American audience, but she did not anticipate what her book
would mean to Samoans decades later. From her perspective,
she had portrayed Samoans in a very positive manner. Yet as Samoans heard about her book or read it in subsequent decades,
a number felt that she had misrepresented them. Her voice was
not their voice. At stake was their identity and their perception
by the wider world.

When Freeman criticized Mead, he claimed to be speaking on
behalf of Samoans, upholding their dignity, pride, and honor. To
him, Mead's book was a "travesty." He was particularly adamant
about the subject that Samoans themselves found most offensive
in Mead's work—her description and interpretation of their private lives. Although *Coming of Age in Samoa* contained only a single chapter about sex contextualized within a broader discussion
of marriage, this part of the book was offensive to a number of
Samoans.

Samoan objections to *Coming of Age in Samoa* were hardly
new. Anthropologist Leonard Mason remembered that, while

using the book in his course at the University of Hawaii in the late 1940s, a young Samoan student protested that, contrary to Mead, Samoans greatly valued female virginity (Freeman 1991: 103) The student, who later became governor of American Samoa, recalled his protest almost four decades later when he appeared in the documentary film *Margaret Mead and Samoa* (1988), a visual summation of Freeman's two books. In 1971, when Mead briefly stopped in American Samoa for her first visit there since the 1920s, a young Samoan woman challenged her on this same issue on local television. Other Samoans, including some Samoan academics, have concurred, believing that Mead did not recognize the significance of virginity and the virtue of Samoan women at the center of their strict public morality. One Samoan academic, Le Tagaloa Fa'anafi, felt that Mead had portrayed Samoans "like animals."

However, other Samoans found Freeman's portrayal of Samoan culture as riddled with conflict, aggression, and rape just as offensive. As Samoan author Albert Wendt wrote, if Mead erred on the side of sexual permissiveness, "Freeman errs on the side of sexual purity, strictness, and abstinence" (1983: 12,14). To Tuaopepe Felix S. Wendt, Freeman's portrayal of Samoans merely replaced one stereotype of the islanders with another in which Samoans were now seen as aggressive and violent (1984).

In the decades following the publication of *Coming of Age in Samoa*, Mead understood her discussion of sex struck a nerve, acknowledging that, had she anticipated that Samoans would read the book, she would have written it differently (1973: preface). And Mead chose not to revise and update the text itself, but rather added prefaces to new editions, explaining that the book should remain faithful to what she observed then and that the islands in the latter decades of the twentieth century were very different than they were in the 1920s (1973: preface).

In the preface to the 1973 edition of *Coming of Age in Samoa*, Mead admitted "my failure to include Samoan young people themselves as possible readers and so address the book to them also, as well as readers of the Western world" (1973: preface). She continued:

Inevitably, young Samoans who read this book will feel somehow not included, because this account of young people two generations ago was written about them, but not for them, as I would write such a book today. But to the students who have the strange experience of having a book about how their ancestors lived . . . I can only say that neither their grandmothers nor I guessed where we would be today . . . . It seems more than ever necessary to stress, shout as loud as I can, this is about Samoa and the United States in 1926–1928. Do not confuse yourselves and the Samoan people by expecting to find life in the Manu'an islands of American Samoa as I found it. (1973: preface)

Today American Samoans experience a very different world than their ancestors in the 1920s. Most do not even live in American Samoa, residing instead in Hawaii and on the American mainland. As U.S. nationals, they can move freely between American Samoa and the rest of the United States. For young Samoans, one avenue for movement is the American military, which recruits heavily in the islands through ROTC and enlistment programs; American Samoa has the highest rate of military enlistment of any U.S. state or territory. Another avenue for mobility is football; college football teams recruit in American Samoa, whose gifted athletes constitute an exceptionally large percentage of U.S. college and professional football team members relative to their actual numbers (Uperesa 2014; Ruck 2018). Other Samoans move abroad for economic reasons and to be with their families in Samoan communities in the diaspora.

Samoan college students in American Samoa and the United States now study their own culture; Samoan academics and authors chronicle cultural persistence and change. There are also challenges for American Samoans in U.S. cities, including poverty and urban gangs that young Samoans sometimes join (T. Sullivan 2005). In the Mead-Freeman controversy, these contemporary realities have often been neglected. Much of the controversy has been conducted in an intellectual time warp as if Samoan culture was somehow eternal and unchanging. For these reasons, the controversy is of little relevance to the lives of Samoans today.

What then has been the value of the controversy? It has encouraged a closer look at the nature of Samoan culture, its history, and transformations, as well as the lives and times of Mead and Freeman. But it has been of little value in situating Mead's accomplishments in historical context, and of no value in terms of advancing theory and method in anthropology. The controversy has lost the immediacy it had when Freeman was alive. After his death in 2001, it gradually faded from public view, but not quite. There are still academics and authors who embrace the hoaxing argument despite readily available and definitive refutations of it, and it continues to survive in corners of the internet where googling the words "liar," "hoax," and "fraud" in association with Margaret Mead is a reminder of the continuing damage to her reputation.

NOTES

Freeman's two books on Mead (1983, 1999) fueled the controversy. For critiques of Freeman, see Shankman (1996, 2006, 2009, 2013), Côté (1994, 2001), Orans (1999), and Holmes (1987) among others. Documentaries on the Mead-Freeman controversy, *Margaret Mead and Samoa* (Heimans 1988) and *Tales from the Jungle: Margaret Mead* (Oxley 2006), can be viewed on the internet. On Freeman, see Hempenstall's (2017) biography and Shankman (2009, 2018c).

1. The first interview with Fa'apua'a was conducted by the son of Fa'apua'a's close friend Fofoa, Galea'i Poumele. Poumele was a high-ranking Samoan chief and administrator in the government of American Samoa who had been corresponding with Freeman and who introduced Freeman to Fa'apua'a. Poumele was familiar with the hoaxing argument and interested in confirming it. At the time of the interview, Fa'apua'a was eighty-six years old, and, before the interview began, Poumele informed her that Mead had written a book in which she slanderously portrayed Samoan adolescent girls as sexually permissive. Fa'apua'a had not previously known of or read *Coming of Age in Samoa*, nor had she known that Mead was an anthropologist. With Freeman present, Poumele then asked Fa'apua'a if she could shed light on how Mead came to this erroneous conclusion.

Poumele framed the interview by telling Fa'apua'a that Mead not only lied about the sexual conduct of adolescent girls but that she had implied that his own mother, Fofoa, was a "slut." (Fofoa had died decades earlier.) Of course, Mead said no such thing, yet Poumele seemed to be bent on obtaining confirmation of the alleged hoaxing. He asked Fa'apua'a if Mead inquired about what she and Fofoa did at night and *if they joked* with her about this. These leading questions were part of the following exchange in what Freeman called the "key excerpt" from the interview:

> *Galea'i Poumele*: Fa'amū, was there a day, a night, or an evening when the woman [i.e., Margaret Mead] questioned you about what you did at nights, and did you ever joke about this?
> *Fa'apua'a Fa'amū*: Yes, we did; we said that we were out at nights with boys; she failed to realize we were just joking and must have been taken in by our pretenses. Yes, she asked: "Where do you go?" And we replied, "We go out at nights!" "With whom?" she asked. Then your mother, Fofoa, and I would pinch each other and say: "We spend the nights with boys, yes, with boys!" She must have taken it seriously but I was only joking. As you know, Samoan girls are terrific liars when it comes to joking. But Margaret Mead accepted our trumped up stories as though they were true. (Freeman 1999:3)

The first interview was relatively brief, and Freeman quoted only this section at the very beginning of the interview, which apparently confirmed that the two Samoan women joked with Mead about their private lives and that Mead genuinely believed that they, "along with other young women of Manu'a, were sexually promiscuous night after night with a succession of different young men" (Freeman 1989:1020). For Freeman, the case for hoaxing was indisputable.

However, Poumele asked additional questions to clarify what Fa'apua'a meant when she said the two women "spend the nights with boys." These questions—more pointed and personal—and her answers were never published. Poumele asked Fa'apua'a directly if Mead had inquired if they were sexually active.

> *Galea'i Poumele*: Did Margaret Mead ask you both, my apologies . . . , whether you had sex with boys at night?
> *Fa'apua'a Fa'amū*: Absolutely not.
> *Galea'i Poumele*: Nothing like that happened to you.
> *Fa'apua'a Fa'amū*: No. Nothing ever happened. (Freeman 1987:2–3)

Thus, when asked directly if Mead asked the women about their private lives, Fa'apua'a said no. If Fa'apua'a did not provide Mead with information about their private lives or the private lives of adolescent girls, how could Mead have been hoaxed?

2. Freeman could have criticized Mead's work in Samoa, revised it, and improved knowledge about Samoan culture without the allegation of hoaxing and without the attribution of self-deception. Yet for Freeman, his exceptional claims about Mead and *Coming of Age in Samoa* were more than academic; they were deeply personal. He saw himself in almost messianic terms, leading a crusade for truth and science against an immoral woman whom he considered a "castrator" and a bully (Barrowclough 1996:37). Freeman was obsessed with Mead, and his critique of her work sometimes reflected deep psychological issues involving women, sex, and dominance (Shankman 2009, 2018c).

CHAPTER 12

LEGACIES

● ● ●

As she entered her sixties and seventies, Mead liked to talk about postmenopausal "zest," a source of personal energy evident even in the last year of her life. Mead's nonstop activities for just the month of January 1978 were recorded by her friend Patricia Grinager as follows:

> *Letters from the Field* [1977] had just been launched. Her column in *Redbook* that month permitted the magazine's readers an early peek at some of her letters from faraway encampments. She was updating *World Enough*, a book that had come out in 1960 with former student Ken Heyman, for republication. She had purchased three round-trip tickets, delivered at least a dozen speeches, and engaged in many professional consultations. She coped with the usual and sometimes annoying adulation that accompanied her live appearances as well as the correspondence that flooded her mail after local and national broadcasts. (1999: 206)

And, at seventy-six, she began teaching three courses at Columbia.

Yet a month later, in February, Mead began to cancel some of her many commitments. She was experiencing symptoms of what would be diagnosed as pancreatic cancer. Yet Mead did not despair. In fact, she was indignant, even defiant, denying the diagnosis and telling those very close to her to keep her declining health a secret even as she was losing sixty pounds. Mead declared that the diagnosis was "nonsense," dismissing the opinions of the several medical specialists that she saw.

Mead would tell colleagues that her weight loss and other symptoms were due to anorexia nervosa or diverticulitis. Although her younger brother had died of pancreatic cancer, Mead, instead of seeking further medical intervention, relied on healer Carmen di Barraza, increasing her visits to Carmen to two or more times a day. Her close relationship with Carmen strained Mead's relationship with her partner Rhoda Métraux., who disapproved of Carmen and wanted Mead to seek more conventional medical treatment. But Mead saw no point in surgery since a diagnosis of pancreatic cancer was terminal.

Metastasis of the cancer and the pain it caused did not deter Mead. She continued teaching, traveling, making appearances, giving talks, and visiting relatives, friends, and colleagues. She was eventually hospitalized, finally succumbing on 15 November 1978.

After Mead's death, there were a number of memorials, including a service at the National Cathedral in Washington, DC, and another at the United Nations. Among her colleagues, Mead was remembered in a special issue of the *American Anthropologist* that included articles on many of the different facets of her life and work. In 2001, on the occasion of Mead's centennial, the annual meetings of the American Anthropological Association featured a two-day symposium with dozens of anthropologists and others reviewing the many dimensions of her work. At these meetings in Washington, DC, anthropologists were invited to visit the Margaret Mead archive at the Library of Congress housing five hundred thousand items that illustrate the breadth of her work and influence. There was also a two-hour public radio program celebrating Mead.

Since her death, there have been biographies of Mead, new editions of her books, collections of her articles and letters, appreciations of Mead, critiques of Mead, documentaries about Mead, books and articles about the Mead-Freeman controversy, and even a U.S. Postal Service stamp commemorating Mead. Her words—"Never doubt that a small group of thoughtful, committed citizens can change the world"—are the most frequently cited quotation by a woman author.

In fiction, a recent bestseller reminded people of Mead's enduring presence. Lily King's award-winning novel *Euphoria* (2014) featured a lead character very similar to Mead conducting fieldwork in the Sepik in the 1930s. Readers, especially women, appreciated the Mead-like character, commenting that they now understood how cultural anthropologists worked, how personal and subjective fieldwork could be, and how ethnography is partially dependent on the personality of the ethnographer.

CONTRIBUTIONS: THEN AND NOW

Mead was prolific and influential. Given her extensive list of accomplishments, there is no single Mead legacy. It may be more helpful to refer to her multiple legacies—determined fieldworker, pioneering ethnographer, methodological innovator, foundational theorist, widely read popularizer, professional leader, and public figure.

Mead studied more different cultures and produced more professional and popular work on them than any other anthropologist in such a brief period of time (1925–1939). She was a relentless fieldworker who actively sought more fieldwork, and more difficult fieldwork, despite her injured ankle, recurring bouts of malaria, frustration, depression, miscarriages, divorces, breakups, new relationships, discrimination, criticism, and professional rejection. Mead did not rest on her early accomplishments although she easily could have. She was too busy seeking new cultures, learning new languages, collecting new kinds of data, and pursuing new ideas. Although Mead's popular books, such as *Coming of Age in Samoa*, remain well known and continue to be read by the public, they are not regarded as essential texts by most contemporary anthropologists. On the other hand, her professional monographs are less well known but demonstrate her ethnographic skills.

Mead was original in her choice of fieldwork topics, initiating research on adolescence, childhood, and gender, and giving them legitimacy in ethnographic inquiry. Critiques and re-evaluations of her work have revised and improved knowledge of these subjects. There is now a substantial anthropological literature on childhood and adolescence in other cultures (Lancy 2008, 2018; Schlegel 1995; Schlegel and Hewett 2011), as well as a large body of work on gender in Melanesia and elsewhere (Strathern 1988; Gewertz and Errington 1987). Each of these subjects, pioneered by Mead, has a much larger literature in disciplines such as biology, psychology, social psychology, and sociology.

During her fifty-two-year career, Mead both witnessed and contributed to the development of anthropology. In the early decades of the twentieth century, "primitive" cultures were thought to be vanishing or, at the very least, being so rapidly absorbed by the modern world that they would be unrecognizable in the near future. The moment for anthropologists to reconstruct the pre-European past was receding. Yet ethnographers like Mead realized that cultures also needed to be studied in the present, as she did in Samoa and New Guinea in the 1920s and the early 1930s, and as they were changing, as on the Omaha reservation in 1930 and on Manus in the 1950s and beyond.

New ways of looking at culture were needed, and Mead's thinking about the relationship between individual personalities and cultural wholes was foundational for one of cultural anthropology's major schools of thought. The ideas that Mead, Benedict, and many others shared about the relationship of culture and personality were provocative and exciting; these studies remain a significant part of the history of American anthropology. But, like most schools of thought in anthropology, they were of a particular time (Bourguignon 1973). The kind of culture and personality studies that Mead originated would be eclipsed, morphing into the broader subdiscipline of psychological anthropology that continues to flourish today.

Mead was a truly innovative thinker, yet she was not known as a great theoretician. She had to put some of her most significant ideas, such as the "squares" and national character, aside.

Mead's most enduring contribution was her early engagement with the concept of culture. Along with Boas and Benedict, she promoted the importance of culture to both academic and public audiences. Due to the scholarship and advocacy of these anthropologists, cultural approaches replaced racial explanations of social differences in the first half of the twentieth century—a major intellectual revolution. Mead provided early ethnographic documentation about the malleability of culture and its cross-cultural variability. Today the concept of culture continues to be vital in both professional and public realms. Although some anthropologists have sought to distance themselves from the concept, in their time Mead, Boas, and Benedict used it to remake the way people thought about humanity.

As a methodological innovator, Mead developed new ways of doing fieldwork. She was among the first to use psychological testing—drawings and projective tests—as well as photography and film in the field. Today, the kinds of psychological testing that Mead and a number of her colleagues employed, as well as the psychoanalytic perspective that accompanied them, have fallen out of favor. However, her early use of photography and film are now recognized as a significant achievement and influence (Jacknis 1988). The annual Margaret Mead Film Festival in New York is part of this legacy.

Mead's concerns about the taking, cataloging, and use of fieldnotes are very contemporary (Sanjek 1990; Sanjek and Tratner 2016). She was adamant that the recording of accurate fieldnotes was essential to successful fieldwork. Mead also emphasized training in field methods that are now part of many graduate programs. The use of laptops has made recording field observations much easier, and the internet now allows frequent communication and feedback between fieldworkers, advisors, and colleagues. Mead would have encouraged all of these developments.

Mead was the first American ethnographer to advocate the use of teams of women and men during fieldwork; she would later recommend that they study the same research topic. For this reason, Mead viewed her earlier fieldwork—resulting in *Coming of Age in Samoa, Growing Up in New Guinea,* and *Sex and Temperament*—as inadequate because, even when working with Reo Fortune, they did not share the same topic. She stated:

[These] are pioneer studies made by a method that I myself would not use again. My future work, like my past three years' work in Bali and among the Iatmul of New Guinea . . . will be cooperative, in which two, or sometimes as many as six, observers armed with modern methods of recording . . . will bring a battery of observation to bear on children or native mothers. (1939: vii)

Mead brought this team-based model to her large-scale studies of national character and to her research on Manus in the 1950s. Her research career thus spanned a continuum from lone village-based ethnographer in Samoa to leader of large interdisciplinary research teams studying national character. Today, despite some notable efforts at team research, most ethnography is still conducted by individual researchers.

The ethics of fieldwork have changed markedly since Mead's early fieldwork, and she would become an important figure in the development of new codes of ethics for field research (Mead 1975). Today fieldwork is far more collaborative and transparent than it was for much of the twentieth century. The people studied are no longer colonial subjects; instead, they are citizens and partners, seeking an active and collaborative voice in the construction of the ethnographic record. Mead considered Unabelin among the Arapesh and John Kilipak on Manus as true research collaborators. Yet in other ways her fieldwork mirrored her times, lacking permissions and internal review boards. Today, informed consent and ethical reviews are mandatory. Fieldwork permissions are often contingent on how the ethnographer's work will contribute to the people that are being studied. Ethnographers are encouraged to consult the people studied about which issues should receive priority in their work. In addition, indigenous scholars now provide accounts of their own cultures, sometimes challenging the work of earlier ethnographers as well as enhancing it. This has been especially true for Mead's work in Samoa and New Guinea.

What set Mead apart from her peers was her ability to make her work relevant to the public by taking conventional wisdom, putting it to the ethnographic test, and drawing lessons for a general audience. She used single, well-documented ethnographic accounts to call into question widely held assumptions about issues of public interest. Thus, she took G. Stanley Hall's assumptions about the universality of adolescent storm and stress and questioned them using Samoan data. She explored Piaget's assumptions about the universality of "primitive" thinking, examining them with information on children in Manus. And she rethought Western assumptions about sex roles, employing ethnographic material from the Arapesh, Mundugumor, and Tchambuli. In writing about these cultures, Mead dared to challenge Americans' own views of themselves.

The way that Mead employed the single case, or a limited number of cases, has been criticized for using "the anecdotal veto" (Wallace 1968: 42). She seemed to be arguing that a single case or instance was all that was needed to negate broader generalizations from a variety of cases. Yet for Mead, mere recognition of cultural differences was the point; she usually did not offer systematic cross-cultural comparisons or detailed explanations of why these differences existed. At the time that Mead was writing up her ethnographic work in the 1920s and 1930s, there were few additional cases for comparison. And, although currently taken for granted, in the early decades of the twentieth century, the mere recognition and understanding of cultural differences were significant lessons for the young discipline of anthropology and the public.

An obvious key to Mead's success with the public was that she wrote in plain English. Mead was proud of *Coming of Age in Samoa* because, as she recalled, it was

> the first piece of anthropological fieldwork which was written without the paraphernalia of scholarship designed to mystify the lay reader and confound one's colleagues. It

seemed to me then—and it still does—that if our studies of the way of life of other people are to be meaningful to the peoples of the industrial world, they must be written for them and not wrapped up in technical jargon for specialists. (1973: preface)

Today there is significant interest in "writing culture" and ethnography as a literary craft, but the specialized vocabularies preferred by cultural anthropologists are geared to professional consumption rather than accessibility to the public. Mead could write for both professional and popular audiences, a rare and valuable skill. She could offer her readers "deliciously literate passages" and "acute images" (Molloy 2009: 341). Using dramatic phrasing to make her points, Mead drew attention, praise, and, of course, criticism.

CONTEMPORARY ASSESSMENTS

During the last three decades of her life, Mead spent most of her time as a public figure—writing, lecturing, networking, leading, and spreading the gospel of anthropology. For anthropology in the public realm, there has been no one else like her. She was the most recognizable American anthropologist of the twentieth century and the most publicly admired. Yet this recognition was often mixed. Conservatives castigated her as hopelessly liberal, while liberals sometimes thought Mead was embarrassingly conservative. Mead herself was so complex—independent, unconventional, paradoxical, and controversial—that it is almost impossible to generalize about her life and work without immediately having to qualify such an assessment.

In recent discussions within anthropology, Mead's name is invariably invoked as an exemplar of what the discipline aspires to be in the public sphere. During her life, though, colleagues often regarded Mead as a "popularizer" who enhanced her own reputation as much as the reputation of anthropology. In their review of Mead's reputation within anthropology in the middle of the twentieth century, Stephen O. Murray and Regna Darnell found that Mead was "widely regarded with contempt as an overheated romancer and popularizer by American anthropologists during the 1950s [and] was not taken seriously as a theorist, even by those who admired her pioneering accumulation of diverse kinds of data" (2000: 570). Mead herself often felt marginalized within anthropology even as her reputation grew in other disciplines and the public realm.

While Mead embodied anthropology for much of the public, for many anthropologists her popularity was cause for ambivalence. John W. Bennett's assessment reflects this concern:

> No anthropologist could equal her for sheer chutzpa and nerve; she was a shameless self-promoter; self-appointed national sales agent for the discipline of anthropology; scourge of various Classic-era anthropologists and their picayune quarrels and preoccupations; a friend and tireless mentor of bright young anthropologists . . . . So what precisely was her role and influence? Her public role is easy to describe: First and foremost was her advocacy of the discipline and her conviction that anthropology had something that the world needed and could use. This certainly instilled confidence in young anthropologists. I recall going to social events and when questioned, admitting that I was an anthropologist, to be met with eager questions about Margaret Mead. She *was* professional identity: and while it was embarrassing to have to say that one had doubts about her probity with respect to research, her name and persona always opened a line of conversation. And, of course, her example was especially important for young women. (1998: 367)

THE MEANING OF MARGARET MEAD

Clifford Geertz, perhaps the most influential cultural anthropologist of the last quarter of the twentieth century, recalled how he and his wife, Hildred, came to their careers as anthropologists

Figure 12.1. Margaret Mead, 1969. Courtesy of the American Museum of Natural History. New York.

in part due to Margaret Mead. In 1950, as young graduates from Antioch College in Ohio, the couple visited Mead in her office at the American Museum of Natural History. They knew very little about anthropology, having majored in philosophy and English respectively. Anthropology was not even taught at Antioch at that time. But, as self-designated "free spirits," they were curious about the discipline and what it might offer them. Mead spent an entire afternoon with the Geertzes, sharing notes, photos, and maps, discussing well-known anthropologists, praising the discipline, and encouraging them to pursue anthropology. As a consequence of that afternoon, Geertz felt "commanded" to become an anthropologist, and the couple soon entered graduate school.

After Mead's death, Geertz was asked to write a biographical essay about her, and he offered a candid review of her work, stating that "some of it was clearly hasty, ill-considered, and casually argued, even irresponsible. Some of it was routine, banal, useful at best, page-filling at worst. Some of it was professional, careful, a modest but genuine addition to knowledge" (1989: 35). But then he added that "some of it was extraordinarily fine, revolutionary when written and revolutionary still" (1989: 335). And, although not known for effusive praise, Geertz concluded by proclaiming, "For my part, I am absolutely astonished (and wildly grateful) that she ever existed in the first place. So, too, the field should be" (1989: 341).

Today doubts that anthropologists had and may still have about Mead and her work have been tempered by recognition of what she accomplished as an anthropologist, as a public figure, and as a woman in a man's world. Yet this positive recognition is relatively recent, occurring in the context of a lower profile and more limited public presence for anthropologists, especially cultural anthropologists, in the public arena. Although there are now a number of initiatives within the discipline explicitly promoting public anthropology, including publication series, websites, blogs, podcasts, articles in professional journals, and awards, these largely serve an internal anthropological constituency rather than a broad public.

The circumstances that allowed Mead to become such an important public figure have changed. Her professional home at the American Museum of Natural History gave her considerable latitude and support in terms of public outreach very early in her career. She was not bound by the constraints of academic anthropology. After World War II, as anthropology grew and gained more exposure, there was an interval during which many anthropologists across the country communicated with a broad public as a normal part of their professional lives. This trend continued into the 1960s and 1970s with anthropologists such as Oscar Lewis, who won the National Book Award for *La Vida* (1972), and Ernest Becker, who won the Pulitzer Prize for *The Denial of Death* (1973), not to mention Mead herself. Commercial publishers were interested in books by anthropologists because they sold well. Many bookstores had separate anthropology sections prominently placed near their entrances, with shelves of books for the general reader.

This bloom faded as anthropologists grew in numbers and became more specialized, as commercial publishing changed, as the criteria for professional advancement became more carefully defined, as the vocabularies that anthropologists used became less comprehensible to the public, and as anthropologists who achieved popular recognition felt the sting of professional criticism and disapproval. Mead herself cast her intellectual net so widely that she was often chastised for speaking and writing outside her presumed areas of competence.

Today, scholars are more cautious about the limits of their expertise. Generalists like Mead have been increasingly replaced by specialists. Anthropology itself has become more like a "holding company" for diverse interests rather than a unified intellectual enterprise. Such specialization is necessary and vital, but it can make communication with general audiences more difficult. Even with the recent interest in public outreach by colleges and universities, such activities are optional. Under these new circumstances, another Margaret Mead is unlikely to emerge.

Anthropologists today want a greater public presence, and this is why Margaret Mead is missed. A recent article was sadly titled "Where Have You Gone, Margaret Mead?" (Sabloff 2011). From the beginning of her career, Mead was unique among American anthropologists in giving priority to studies that informed our daily lives. In writing about Samoa and the other cultures that she studied, she believed that anthropology was ideally suited to the understanding of contemporary issues in America. As she stated just prior to the publication of *Coming of Age in Samoa* in 1928, "By the study and analysis of the diverse solutions that confront us today, it is possible to make a more reasoned judgment of the needs of our own society" (1927b: 467–68). Mead set her agenda accordingly and lived by these words for the rest of her life.

SELECTED WORKS
BY MARGARET MEAD

● ● ●

1928. *Coming of Age in Samoa: A Psychological Study of Primitive Youth for Western Civilisation.* New York: William Morrow.

1930. *Growing Up in New Guinea.* New York: William Morrow.

1932. *The Changing Culture of an Indian Tribe.* New York: Columbia University Press.

1935. *Sex and Temperament in Three Primitive Societies.* New York: William Morrow.

1942. *Balinese Character: A Photographic Analysis.* A Special Publication of the New York Academy of Sciences, vol. 2. New York: New York Academy of Sciences. (Edited with Gregory Bateson.)

1949. *Male and Female: A Study of the Sexes in a Changing World.* New York: William Morrow.

1953. *The Study of Culture at a Distance.* Chicago: University of Chicago Press. (Edited with Rhoda Métraux.)

1956. *New Lives for Old: Cultural Transformation—Manus, 1928–1953.* New York: William Morrow and Co.

1972. *Blackberry Winter: My Earlier Years.* New York: Pocket Books.

1977. *Letters from the Field, 1925–1975.* New York: Harper and Row.

2006. *To Cherish the Life of the World: Selected Letters of Margaret Mead.* New York: Basic Books. (Edited by Margaret M. Caffrey and Patricia A. Francis.)

REFERENCES

• • •

AUDIOVISUAL MATERIALS

Gullahorn-Holecek, Barbara, dir. 1983. "Papua New Guinea: Anthropology on Trial." *NOVA*, 1 November 1983, PBS.

Bateson, Gregory, and Margaret Mead, dirs. 1952. *Trance and Dance in Bali*. Documentary.

Donahue, Phil, prod. 1983. Interview with Derek Freeman. *Donahue*, 18 March 1983, CBS.

Gilbert, Craig, dir. 1968. *Margaret Mead's New Guinea Journal*. Documentary, PBS.

Heimans, Frank. dir. 1988. *Margaret Mead and Samoa*. Documentary.

Oxley, Peter, dir. 2006. *Tales from the Jungle: Margaret Mead*. Documentary, BBC.

Peck, Ann, dir. 1981. *Margaret Mead: Taking Note*. Documentary, BBC Odyssey Series.

Robertson, Nancy, prod. 2001. "To Cherish the Life of the World: 100 Years of Margaret Mead." *Diane Rehm Show*, 16 December 2001, National Public Radio.

PRINTED MATERIALS

Banner, Lois W. 2003. *Intertwined Lives: Margaret Mead, Ruth Benedict, and Their Circle*. New York: Knopf.

———. 2004. "The Bo-Cu Plant: Ruth Benedict and Gender." In *Reading Benedict / Reading Mead: Feminism, Race, and Imperial Visions*, edited by Dolores Janiewski and Lois W. Banner, 16–32. Baltimore: Johns Hopkins University Press.

Barrowclough, Nikki. 1996. "Sex, Lies, and Anthropology." *Sydney Morning Herald Magazine*, 9 March 1996, 31–39.

Bateson, Gregory. 1936. *Naven: A Survey of the Problems Suggested by a Composite Picture of the Culture of a New Guinea Tribe Drawn from Three Points of View*. Cambridge: Cambridge University Press.

Bateson, Gregory, and Margaret Mead. 1942. *Balinese Character: A Photographic Analysis*. A Special Publication of the New York Academy of Sciences, vol. 2. New York: New York Academy of Sciences.

Bateson, Mary Catherine. 1984. *With a Daughter's Eye: A Memoir of Margaret Mead and Gregory Bateson*. New York: William Morrow.

Boas, Franz. 1911. *The Mind of Primitive Man*. New York: Macmilllan.

Bourguignon, Erika. 1973. "Psychological Anthropology." In *Handbook of Social and Cultural Anthropology*, edited by John J. Honigmann, 1073–1118. Chicago: Rand McNally and Co.

Benedict, Ruth. 1934. *Patterns of Culture*. Boston: Houghton Mifflin.

———. 1946. *The Chrysanthemum and the Sword*. New York: World Publishing.

Bennett, John W. 1998. *Classic Anthropology*. New Brunswick, NJ: Transaction Publishers.

Becker, Ernest. 1973. *The Denial of Death*. New York: Basic Books.

Bloom, Allan. 1987. *The Closing of the American Mind: How Higher Education Has Failed Democracy and Impoverished the Souls of Today's Students*. New York: Simon and Schuster.

Blum, Deborah Beatriz. 2017. *Coming of Age: The Sexual Awakening of Margaret Mead*. New York: St. Martin's Press.

Boochani, Behrouz. 2019. *No Friend but the Mountains: Writing from Manus Prison*. Toronto: House of Anansi Press.

Caffrey, Margaret M., and Patricia A. Francis, eds. 2006. *To Cherish the Life of the World: Selected Letters of Margaret Mead*. New York: Basic Books.

Coontz, Stephanie. 2011. *A Strange Stirring: The Feminist Mystique and American Women at the Dawn of the 1960s*. New York: Basic Books.

Côté, James E. 1994. *Adolescent Storm and Stress: An Evaluation of the Mead-Freeman Controversy*. Hillsdale, NJ: Lawrence Erlbaum Associates.

———. 2000. "Was *Coming of Age in Samoa* Based on a 'Fateful Hoaxing'? A Close Look at Freeman's Claim Based on the Mead-Boas Correspondence." *Current Anthropology* 41(4): 617–620.

———. 2005. "The Correspondence Associated with Margaret Mead's Samoa Research: What Does It Really Tell Us?" *Pacific Studies* 28(3/4): 60–73.

Cressman, Luther Sheeleigh. 1988. *A Golden Journey: Memoirs of an Archaeologist*. Salt Lake City: University of Utah Press.

Darnell, Regna 1990. *Edward Sapir: Linguist, Anthropologist, Humanist.* Berkeley: University of California Press.

di Leonardo, Micaela. 1998. *Exotics at Home: Anthropologies, Others, American Modernity.* Chicago: University of Chicago Press.

Dillon, Wilton. 1980. "Margaret Mead and Government." *American Anthropologist* 82(2): 319–339.

Dobrin, Lise M., and Ira Bashkow. 2006. "Pigs for Dance Songs": Reo Fortune's Empathetic Ethnography of the Arapesh Road." *Histories of Anthropology Annual* 2: 123–154.

———. 2010a. "'The Truth in Anthropology Does Not Travel First Class': Reo Fortune's Fateful Encounter with Margaret Mead." *Histories of Anthropology Annual* 6: 66–128.

———. 2010b. "Arapesh Warfare": Reo Fortune's Veiled Critique of Margaret Mead's Sex and Temperament." *American Anthropologist* 112(3): 370–383.

Eggan, Fred. 1968. "One Hundred Years of Ethnology and Social Anthropology." In *One Hundred Years of Anthropology*, edited by J. O. Brew, 116–149. Cambridge, MA: Harvard University Press.

Foerstel, Lenora, and Angela Gilliam, eds. 1992. *Confronting the Margaret Mead Legacy: Scholarship, Empire, and the South Pacific.* Philadelphia: Temple University Press.

Francis, Patricia A. 2001. "'Something to Think With': Mead, Psychology, and the Road to Samoa." Unpublished manuscript prepared for the annual meeting of the Association for Social Anthropology in Oceania, Miami, FL, 16 February 2001.

———. 2005. "Margaret Mead and Psychology: The Education of an Anthropologist." *Pacific Studies* 28(3/4): 74–90.

Freeman, Derek. 1948. "The Social Organization of a Samoan Village Community." Postgraduate Diploma Thesis in Anthropology. London School of Economics.

———. 1983. *Margaret Mead and Samoa: The Making and Unmaking of an Anthropological Myth.* Cambridge, MA: Harvard University Press.

———. 1987. "Interview 1 with Fa'apua'a Fa'amū." In Derek Freeman Papers, 1940–2001, Mandeville Special Collections Library in the Geisel Library, University of California, San Diego.

———. 1991. "There's Tricks i' th' World: An Historical Analysis of the Samoan Researches of Margaret Mead." *Visual Anthropology Review* 7(1): 103–128.

———. 1999. *The Fateful Hoaxing of Margaret Mead: A Historical Analysis of Her Samoan Research.* Boulder: Westview Press.

Friedan, Betty. 1963. *The Feminine Mystique.* New York: Dell.

Geertz, Clifford. 1989. "Margaret Mead: December 16, 1901 – November 15, 1978." In *Biographical Memoirs*, edited by the National Academy of Sciences, vol. 58, 329–354. Washington, DC: National Academy of Sciences Press.

Gewertz, Deborah. 1981. "A Historical Reconsideration of Female Dominance among the Chambri of Papua New Guinea." *American Ethnologist* 8(1): 94–106.

———. 1984. "The Tchambuli View of Persons: A Critique of Individualism in the Works of Mead and Chodorow." *American Anthropologist* 86(3): 615–629.

Gewertz, Deborah, and Frederick Errington. 1987. *Cultural Alternatives and a Feminist Anthropology: An Analysis of Culturally Constructed Gender Interests in Papua New Guinea*. New York: Cambridge University Press.

Gilkeson, John S. 2009. "Clyde Kluckhohn and the New Anthropology: From Culture and Personality to the Scientific Study of Values." *Pacific Studies* 32(2/3): 251–272.

Gilliam, Angela. 1992. "Leaving a Record for Others: An Interview with Nahau Rooney." In *Confronting the Margaret Mead Legacy: Scholarship, Empire, and the South Pacific*, edited by Lenora Foerstel and Angela Gilliam, 31–54. Philadelphia: Temple University Press.

Gordan, Joan, ed. 1976. *Margaret Mead: The Complete Bibliography 1925–1975*. The Hague: Mouton.

Gorer, Geoffrey. 1938. *Himalayan Village: An Account of the Lepchas of Sikkim*. London: M. Joseph, Ltd.

———. 1961. "The Concept of National Character." In *Personality in Nature, Society, and Culture*, edited by C. Kluckhohn and H. A. Murray, 246–259. New York: Alfred A. Knopf.

Gorer, Geoffrey, and John Rickman. 1949. *The People of Great Russia: A Psychological Study*. London: Cresset Press.

Grinager, Patricia. 1999. *Uncommon Lives: My Lifelong Friendship with Margaret Mead*. Lanham, MD: Rowman & Littlefield Publishers, Inc.

Hall, G. Stanley. 1904. *Adolescence: Its Psychology and Its Relations to Physiology, Anthropology, Sociology, Sex, Crime, Religion, and Education*. New York: D. Appleton and Co.

Harris, Marvin. 1968. *The Rise of Anthropological Theory*. New York: Crowell.

Hempenstall, Peter J. 2017. *Truth's Fool: Derek Freeman and the War over Cultural Anthropology*. Madison: University of Wisconsin Press.

Hart, C. W. M. 1932. "Review of *Growing Up in New Guinea* by Margaret Mead." *Man* 32:146.

Henry, Jules. 1963. *Culture against Man*. New York: Random House.

Herdt, Gilbert, and Stephen C. Leavitt, eds. 1998. *Adolescence in Pacific Island Societies*. Pittsburgh: University of Pittsburgh Press.

Hinton, Peter. 2002. "The 'Thailand Controversy' Revisited." *Australian Journal of Anthropology* 13(2): 155–177.

Holmes, Lowell D. 1987. *Quest for the Real Samoa: The Mead/Freeman Controversy and Beyond*. South Hadley, MA: Bergin and Garvey.

Honigmann, John J. 1967. *Personality in Culture*. New York: Harper and Row.

Howard, Jane. 1984. *Margaret Mead: A Life*. New York: Fawcett Crest.

Iamo, Warilea. 1992. "The Stigma of New Guinea: Reflections on Anthropology and Anthropologists." In *Confronting the Margaret Mead Legacy: Scholarship, Empire, and the South Pacific*, edited by Lenora Foerstel and Angela Gilliam, 75–100. Philadelphia: Temple University Press.

Inkeles, Alex. 1961. "National Character and Modern Political Systems." In *Psychological Anthropology: Approaches to Culture and Personality*, edited by F. L. K. Hsu, 172–208. Homewood, Il: Dorsey Press.

Jacknis, Ira. 1988. "Margaret Mead and Gregory Bateson in Bali: Their Use of Photography and Film." *Cultural Anthropology* 3(2): 160–177.

Janiewski, Dolores. 2001. "Margaret Mead and the Ambiguities of Sexual Citizenship for Women." In *Women's Rights and Human Rights*, edited by Patricia Grimshaw, Katie Holmes, and Marilyn Lake, 105–120. London: Palgrave Macmillan.

Jonsson, Hjorleifur. 2014. "Phantom Scandal: On the National Uses of the 'Thailand Controversy.'" *Sojourn: Journal of Social Issues in Southeast Asia* 29(2): 263–299.

King, Charles. 2019. *Gods of the Upper Air: How a Circle of Renegade Anthropologists Reinvented Race, Sex, and Gender in the Twentieth Century*. New York: Doubleday.

King, Lily. 2014. *Euphoria*. New York: Atlantic Monthly Press.

Kroeber, Alfred. 1931. "Review of *Growing Up in New Guinea* by Margaret Mead." *American Anthropologist* 33(2): 248–250.

Lancy, David F. 2008. *The Anthropology of Childhood: Cherubs, Chattel, Changelings*. Cambridge: Cambridge University Press.

———. 2018. *Anthropological Perspectives on Children as Helpers, Workers, Artisans, and Laborers*. New York: Palgrave.

Lapsley, Hilary. 1999. *Margaret Mead and Ruth Benedict: The Kinship of Women*. Amherst: University of Massachusetts Press.

LeVine, Robert A. 1973. *Culture, Behavior, and Personality*. Chicago: Aldine.

Lewis, Herbert S. 2014. *In Defense of Anthropology: An Investigation of the Critique of Anthropology*. New Brunswick, NJ: Transaction Press.

Lewis, Oscar. 1972. *La Vida: A Puerto Rican Family in the Culture of Poverty—San Juan and New York*. New York: Random House.

Lutkehaus, Nancy C. 2008. *Margaret Mead: American Icon*. Princeton: Princeton University Press.

Mandler, Peter. 2009. "One World, Many Cultures: Margaret Mead and the Limits of Cold War Anthropology." *History Workshop Journal* 68(1): 149–172.

———. 2013. *Return from the Natives: How Margaret Mead Won the Second World War and Lost the Cold War*. New Haven: Yale University Press.

McDowell, Edwin. 1990. "New Samoa Book Challenges Margaret Mead's Conclusions." In *The Samoa Reader: Anthropologists Take Stock*, edited by H. Caton, 211–216. Lanham, MD: University Press of America.

———. 1991. *The Mundugumor: From the Field Notes of Margaret Mead and Reo Fortune*. Washington, DC: Smithsonian Institution Press.

Mead, Margaret. 1924. "Intelligence Tests of Italian and American Children." Master's thesis, Department of Psychology, Columbia University, New York.

———. 1927a. "The Adolescent Girl in Samoa. Report to the National Research Council." Manuscript. Library of Congress.

———. 1927b. "The Need for Teaching Anthropology in Normal Schools and Teachers' Colleges." *School and Society* 26(667): 466–469.

———. (1928a) 1969. *An Inquiry into the Question of Cultural Stability in Polynesia*. Columbia University Contributions to Anthropology, vol. 9. New York: AMS Press.

———. (1928b) 1973. *Coming of Age in Samoa: A Psychological Study of Primitive Youth for Western Civilisation*. New York: William Morrow.

———. 1930a. "Social Organization of Manu'a." *Bernice P. Bishop Museum Bulletin* 76.

———. (1930b) 1960. *Growing Up in New Guinea*. New York: William Morrow.

———. (1932) 1965. *The Changing Culture of an Indian Tribe*. New York: Columbia University Press.

———. 1933. "More Comprehensive Field Methods." *American Anthropologist* 35(1): 1–15.

———. 1934. *Kinship in the Admiralty Islands*. Anthropological Papers of the American Museum of Natural History, vol. 34, part 2. New York: American Museum of Natural History.

———. 1935. *Sex and Temperament in Three Primitive Societies*. New York: William Morrow.

———. 1937a. "A Reply to a Review of *Sex and Temperament in Three Primitive Societies*." *American Anthropologist* 39(3): 558–561.

———, ed. 1937b. *Cooperation and Competition among Primitive Peoples*. New York: McGraw-Hill.

———. 1938. *The Mountain Arapesh*. Vol. 1, *An Importing Culture*. Anthropological Papers of the American Museum of Natural History. New York: American Museum of Natural History.

———. 1939. *From the South Seas: Studies of Adolescence and Sex in Primitive Societies*. New York: William Morrow.

———. 1940. *The Mountain Arapesh*. Vol. 2, *Supernaturalism*. Anthropological Papers of the American Museum of Natural History. New York: American Museum of Natural History.

———. 1942a. "Balinese Character." In *Balinese Character: A Photographic Analysis*, edited by Gregory Bateson and Margaret Mead. A Special Publication of the New York Academy of Sciences, vol. 2. New York: New York Academy of Sciences.

———. 1942b. *And Keep Your Powder Dry: An Anthropologist Looks at America*. New York: W. Morrow and Co.

———. 1949. *Male and Female: A Study of the Sexes in a Changing World*. New York: William Morrow.

———. 1951a. *Soviet Attitudes towards Authority*. New York: McGraw-Hill.

———. 1951b. *The School in American Culture*. Cambridge, MA: Harvard University Press.

———. 1952. "Foreword." In *Life Is with People: The Culture of the Shtetl*, edited by Mark Zborowski and Elizabeth Herzog, 11–21. New York: Schocken.

———. 1954. "The Swaddling Hypothesis: Its Reception." *American Anthropologist* 56(3): 395–409.

———, ed. 1955. *Cultural Patterns and Technical Change*. New York: UNESCO.

———. 1956. *New Lives for Old: Cultural Transformation—Manus, 1928–1953*. New York: William Morrow and Co.

———. 1959. *An Anthropologist at Work: Writings of Ruth Benedict*. Boston: Houghton Mifflin Company.

———. 1961. "Anthropology among the Sciences." *American Anthropologist* 63(3): 475–482.

———. 1964. *Continuities in Cultural Evolution*. New Haven, CT: Yale University Press.

———. (1965a) 2000. "Preface – 1965." In *And Keep Your Powder Dry: An Anthropologist Looks at America*, xxxi–xxxiii. New York: Berghahn.

———. (1965b) 2000. "Introduction." In *And Keep Your Powder Dry: An Anthropologist Looks at America*, xxvix–xlii. New York: Berghahn.

———. 1968. *The Mountain Arapesh*. New York: American Museum of Natural History Press.

———. 1970. *Culture and Commitment: A Study of the Generation Gap*. New York: Doubleday.

———. 1972. *Blackberry Winter: My Earlier Years*. New York: Pocket Books.

———. 1975. "The Evolving Ethics of Applied Anthropology." In *Applied Anthropology in America*, edited by Elizabeth M. Eddy and William L. Partridge, 425–437. New York: Columbia University Press.

———. 1976. "Towards a Human Science." *Science* 191(4230): 903–909.

———. 1977. *Letters from the Field, 1925–1975*. New York: Harper & Row.

Mead, Margaret, and James Baldwin. 1971. *A Rap on Race*. Philadelphia: J. B. Lippincott.

Mead, Margaret, and Paul Byers. 1968. *The Small Conference: An Innovation in Communication*. Paris: Mouton.

Mead, Margaret, and Ken Heyman. 1960. *World Enough: Rethinking the Future*. Boston: Little Brown.

Mead, Margaret, and Frances Balgley Kaplan, eds. 1965. *American Women*. New York: Charles Scribner's Sons.

Mead, Margaret, and Francis Cooke Macgregor. 1951. *Growth and Culture: A Photographic Study of Balinese Character*. New York: G. P. Putnam's Sons.

Mead, Margaret, and Rhoda Métraux. 1978. *An Interview with Santa Claus*. New York: Walker & Co.

Molloy, Maureen. 2008. *On Creating a Usable Culture: Margaret Mead and the Emergence of American Cosmopolitanism*. Honolulu: University of Hawai'i Press.

———. 2009. "'More Like Fighting Than Waiting': Mead, Method, and the Proper Object of Knowledge in Anthropology." *Pacific Studies* 32(2/3): 325–347.

Murray, Stephen O., and Regna Darnell. 2000. "Margaret Mead and Paradigm Shifts within Anthropology during the 1920s." *Journal of Youth and Adolescence* 29(5): 557–573.

Orans, Martin. 1996. *Not Even Wrong: Margaret Mead, Derek Freeman, and the Samoans*. Novato, CA: Chandler and Sharp.

———. 2000. "Hoaxing, Polemics, and Science." *Current Anthropology* 41(4): 615–616.

Petersen, Glenn. 2015. "American Anthropology's 'Thailand Contro-versy': An Object Lesson in Professional Responsibility." *Sojourn: Journal of Social Issues in Southeast Asia* 30(2): 528–549.

Price, David H. 2008. *Anthropological Intelligence: The Deployment and Neglect of American Anthropology in the Second World War*. Durham, NC: Duke University Press.

———. 2016. *Cold War Anthropology: The CIA, The Pentagon, and the Growth of Dual Use Anthropology*. Durham: Duke University Press.

Roscoe, Paul. 2003. "Margaret Mead, Reo Fortune, and Mountain Ara-pesh Warfare." *American Anthropologist* 105(3): 581–591.

Ruck, Robert. 2018. *Tropic of Football: The Long and Perilous Journey of Samoans to the NFL*. New York: New Press.

Sabloff, Jeremy. 2011. "Where Have You Gone Margaret Mead? Anthro-pology and Public Intellectuals." *American Anthropologist* 113(3): 408–416.

Sanjek, Roger, ed. 1990. *Fieldnotes: The Makings of Anthropology*. Ithaca: Cornell University Press.

Sanjek, Roger, and Susan W. Tratner, eds. 2016. *eFieldnotes: The Mak-ings of Anthropology in the Digital Age*. Philadelphia. University of Pennsylvania Press.

Sapir, Edward. 1929a. "The Discipline of Sex." *American Mercury* 16: 413–420.

———. 1929b "The Unconscious Patterning of Behavior in Society." In *The Unconscious: A Symposium*, edited by C. M. Child et al., 114–142. New York: A. A. Knopf.

Schlegel, Alice. 1991. "Status, Property, and the Value on Virginity." *American Ethnologist* 18(4): 719–734.

———. 1995. "The Cultural Management of Adolescent Sexuality." In *Sexual Nature/Sexual Culture*, edited by P. R. Abramson and S. D. Pinkerton, 177–194. Chicago: University of Chicago Press.

Schlegel, Alice, and Herbert Barry III. 1991. *Adolescence: An Anthropo-logical Inquiry*. New York: Free Press.

Schlegel, Alice, and Barry Hewlett. 2011. "Contributions of Anthropol-ogy to the Study of Adolescence." *Journal of Research on Adolescence* 2(1): 281–289.

Shankman, Paul. 1996. "The History of Samoan Sexual Conduct and the Mead-Freeman Controversy." *American Anthropologist* 98(3): 555–567.

———. 2005. "Margaret Mead's Other Samoa: Rereading *Social Orga-nization of Manu'a*." *Pacific Studies* 28(3/4): 46–59.

———. 2006. "Virginity and Veracity: Re-reading Historical Sources in the Mead-Freeman Controversy." *Ethnohistory* 53(3): 478–505.

———. 2009. *The Trashing of Margaret Mead: Anatomy of an Anthropological Controversy*. Madison: University of Wisconsin Press.

———. 2013. "The 'Fateful Hoaxing' of Margaret Mead: A Cautionary Tale." *Current Anthropology* 54(1): 51–69.

———. 2018a. "Margaret Mead." In *Anthropology*, edited by John P. Jackson Jr. Oxford Online Bibliography. New York: Oxford University Press.

———. 2018b. "The Public Anthropology of Margaret Mead: *Redbook*, Women's Issues, and the 1960s." *Current Anthropology* 59(1): 55–73.

———. 2018c. "In Search of Derek Freeman." *Reviews in Anthropology* 47(3/4): 57–75.

Silverman, Sydel. 2004. "Margaret Mead." In *Totems and Teachers: Key Figures in the History of Anthropology*, 2nd edition, edited by Sydel Silverman, 206–220. New York: Alta Mira Press.

Spindler, George P., ed. 1978. *The Making of Psychological Anthropology*. Berkeley: University of California Press.

Strathern, Marilyn. 1988. *The Gender of the Gift*. Berkeley: University of California Press.

Sullivan, Gerald. 1999. *Margaret Mead, Gregory Bateson and Highland Bali: Fieldwork Photographs of Bayung Gedé*. Chicago: University of Chicago Press.

———. 2004. "A Four-Fold Humanity: Margaret Mead and Psychological Types." *Journal of the History of the Behavioral Sciences* 40(2): 183–206.

———. 2009. "Of External Habits and Maternal Attitudes: Margaret Mead, Gestalt Psychology, and the Reproduction of Character." *Pacific Studies* 32 (2/3): 222–250.

Sullivan, Tim. 2005. "The Gangs of Zion." *High Country News* 37(14): 9–17.

Time magazine. 1969. "Margaret Mead Today: Mother to the World." 21 March 1969.

Thomas, Caroline. 2009. "Rediscovering Reo: Reflections on the Life and Anthropological Career of Reo Franklin Fortune." *Pacific Studies* 32(2/3): 299–324.

Thurnwald, Richard C. 1936. "Review of *Sex and Temperament in Three Primitive Societies*." *American Anthropologist* 38(4): 663–667.

Tuzin, Donald F., and Theodore Schwartz. 1980. "Margaret Mead in New Guinea: An Appreciation." *Oceania* 50(4): 241–247.

Uperesa, F. L. 2014. "Fabled Futures: Migration and Mobility for Samoans in American Football." *Contemporary Pacific* 26(2): 281–300.

Wakin, Eric. 1992. *Anthropology Goes to War: Professional Ethics and Counterinsurgency in Thailand*. University of Wisconsin Center for Southeast Asian Studies Monograph 7. Madison: University of Wisconsin.

Wallace, Anthony F. C. 1952. *The Modal Personality Structure of the Tuscarora Indians as Revealed by the Rorschach Test*. Bureau of American Ethnology. Washington, DC: Smithsonian Institution.

———. 1961. *Culture and Personality*. Random House.

———. 1968. "Anthropological Contributions to the Theory of Personality." In *The Study of Personality: An Interdisciplinary Appraisal*, edited by Edward Norbeck, Douglass Price-Williams, and William McCord, 41–53. New York: Holt, Rinehart and Winston.

Wendt, Albert. 1983. "Three Faces of Samoa: Mead's, Freeman's, and Wendt's." *Pacific Islands Monthly*, April 1983, 10–14, 69.

Wendt, Tuaopepe Felix S. 1984. "Review of Derek Freeman: *Margaret Mead and Samoa: The Making and Unmaking of an Anthropological Myth*." *Pacific Studies* 7(2): 91–99.

Yans-McLaughlin, Virginia. 1986a. "Mead, Bateson, and 'Hitler's Peculiar Psychological Makeup'—Applying Anthropology in the Era of Appeasement." *History of Anthropology Newsletter* 8(1): 3–8.

———. 1986b. "Science, Democracy, and Ethics: Mobilizing Culture and Personality for World War II." In *Malinowski, Rivers, Benedict and Others: Essays on Culture and Personality*, edited by George Stocking Jr., 184–217. Madison: University of Wisconsin Press.

Yans, Virginia. 2004. "On the Political Anatomy of Mead-Bashing, or Re-thinking Margaret Mead." In *Reading Benedict / Reading Mead: Feminism, Race, and Imperial Visions*, edited by Dolores Janiewski and Lois W. Banner, 229–248. Baltimore: Johns Hopkins University Press, 2004.

INDEX

● ● ●

110, 111–12; research teams, 155; Thurnwald and, 71. See also *Growing Up in New Guinea* (Mead); *and specific groups of people*

New Lives for Old (Mead), 110

Office of Secret Services (OSS), 89, 94
Ogburn, William Fielding, 12, 32
Omaha reservation, 50–53, 123
Orans, Martin, 143
organizations, and Mead: AAA, 76, 116, 119, 140, 151; American Association for the Advancement of Science, 4, 116, 140; Delos Symposium, 116; HEW, 117, 118, 129; Human Lactation Center, 116; Institute for Intercultural Studies, 116; National Research Council, 16, 19, 31, 32, 33, 36, 40, 75; National Research Council, Committee on Food Habits, 87, 89, 92–93; Scientists' Institute for Public Information, 116; Society for Applied Anthropology, 3, 92, 116; Society for General Systems Research, 116; Storefront Community School board, 116; World Council of Churches, 116; World Foundation for Mental Health, 116; World Society for Ekistics, 116
OSS (Office of Secret Services), 89, 94

Papua New Guinea, 110, 111–12. *See also* New Guinea; *and specific groups of people*
Parsons, Talcott, 94
Patterns of Culture (Benedict), 58, 73, 76, 96
peace efforts, 86, 90, 91, 94, 96, 97, 102, 122
Piaget, Jean, 46, 156

Pinker, Steven, 140
politics, 86, 87, 89–90, 97, 102, 103, 117–18
postwar years, and Mead: culture and personality studies, 96–97; interdisciplinary research, 3–4, 96–97, 98; Manus, 107–8; national character studies, 95–97. *See also* World War II
The President's Commission on the Status of Women, 129, 130
psychoanalysis, 9, 57, 74, 77, 101, 117
psychological tests, and fieldwork, 10, 11–12, 23, 43, 57, 59, 107
public figure/role, and Mead: activism, 6, 35, 116–18, 124; amplification/cultivation of, 104, 113–14; anthropology, 2, 4, 5, 42, 77, 157–58, 161; climate change, 116–17; critiques, 4, 5, 121–22, 157–58, 161; described, 4, 53, 104, 113–14; Equal Rights Amendment, 127, 133; feminism, 4, 37, 70, 104; on the future, 116, 122–24; globalism, 122–23; influential thinker, 4, 94, 102, 126, 134–35, 152, 157; lecturer, 53, 93, 113–14, 117; legacies, 1, 160–61; Mead-Baldwin dialogue, 124, 125; Mead Report, 120–22; "Mother to the World" title, 4; news stories, 53, 113, 134; peace efforts, 86, 90, 91, 94, 97, 122; political figures and, 1, 118, 119, 129, 131; politics, 86, 87, 117–18, 119–20, 121, 122, 123; race relations, 124–25; radio broadcasts, 4, 92, 93, 113–14; sexual revolution, 4, 132, 133; television programs, 4, 113, 124; Thailand controversy, 120–22; Vietnam War, 119–22, 123; women's issues, 126–27; women's movement, 4, 70–71; World War II, 86–87, 89, 92–93, 94, 95;

www.ingramcontent.com/pod-product-compliance
Lightning Source LLC
Chambersburg PA
CBHW070930030426
42336CB00014BA/2605